WHAT YOUR COLLEAGUES ARE SAYING . . .

"In a world that often feels disconnected, developing SEL Muscles is more essential than ever for fostering meaningful connections and promoting healthy relationships—with both others and ourselves. This book masterfully combines evidence-based practices and research to present six critical tools for personal growth. Lori Woodley-Langendorff draws on the expertise of specialists, seamlessly blending neuroscience with practical, actionable steps to help readers enhance their lives."

—Raghu Appasani, MD
Integrative and Addiction Psychiatrist and Entrepreneur

"In SEL Muscle Mastery, *Lori offers a revolutionary approach to building emotional strength and fostering connection. Her six tools are not just strategies—they are life-changing practices that align perfectly with living your passions and creating meaningful relationships. This book is an essential guide for anyone ready to make a difference in their own life and the lives of others."*

—Janet Bray Attwood
New York Times Bestselling Author, Trainer, Humanitarian

"With over thirty years of experience in education, I've never seen a greater need for schools to be equipped with tools that address social-emotional learning. I believe we have yet to fully recognize the long-term impact COVID has had on children, and how these effects continue to manifest even five years later. This book is rooted in solid research, with tools that Lori's team has successfully used to demonstrate effective strategies and practices that can be easily applied in classrooms. I am grateful for Lori's expertise and collaboration with our school, and I am thrilled that others will now benefit from her valuable insights."

—Dr. Marlene Batista
Superintendent, Los Angeles, CA

"As a child and family therapist, I'm often asked for quick, effective solutions that deliver immediate results. This book provides exactly that—a practical, accessible guide to better understanding yourself through six core SEL Muscles. The book includes relatable examples from both classroom and home settings, and it breaks down each concept into actionable steps, empowering readers to become stronger leaders, clearer communicators, and more thoughtful problem-solvers in their families, classrooms, and communities. Each SEL Muscle builds on essential skills like empathy, accountability, and curiosity, offering tools that are not only easy to apply but also profoundly effective. By consistently flexing these muscles, readers can create lasting, meaningful change in their relationships and inspire those around them to grow as well."

—Sarah Bernson, LMFT
Child and Family Therapist, Trauma Therapist,
and SEL Trainer and Facilitator

*"*SEL Muscle Mastery *is a game-changer for educators and parents seeking practical strategies to strengthen emotional resilience and create a more balanced life. With relatable insights and actionable techniques, this book equips readers with six essential mental muscles to navigate challenges with confidence and ease. It's a must-read for anyone committed to fostering emotional intelligence and well-being in themselves and the children they support!"*

—LaDonna Braswell, EdS
High School Principal, Jackson, Tennessee

"The topic in SEL Muscle Mastery *is timely, and I appreciate the manner in which Lori Woodley-Langendorff looks at the whole person AND the whole community. The author's passion and personal stake are evident. They are honest that there can be pitfalls and difficulties, but that the benefits make up for the struggle.*

Woodley-Langendorff shows the reader that flexing your muscles doesn't just happen in the gym: in fact, we exercise our brains and bodies almost daily, yet we often fail to recognize the necessity in stretching our social and emotional skills. SEL Muscle Mastery *makes the case for not only the existence of SEL muscles, but the importance of growing them with intentionality."*

—Melissa A. Campbell
K-5 Mathematics Specialist,
Alabama Math, Science, and Technology (AMSTI):
University of Alabama at Huntsville, AL

"Most of us accept the gloom and doom about our school systems: disengaged staff, outdated methods, and the countless safety concerns of students—and not just physical safety, but emotional and psychological safety as well. Instead of accepting the status quo, Lori Woodley-Langendorff has written a manifesto. These are the six mental muscles educators must build not only to teach our next generation, but also to have more fun doing it. Her ideas are battle-tested daily, in her living laboratory of storytelling, filmmaking, and creating movements with educators across the globe. If you got in the game to create safe spaces for your students to thrive, this is your book."

—Kristoffer Carter
Best-Selling Author of *Permission to Glow: A Spiritual Guide to Epic Leadership*

"SEL Muscle Mastery *is an essential tool kit for anyone committed to nurturing resilience and connection for young people. This book expertly blends relatable stories and practical insights with transformative approaches, making it a must-read for educators and caregivers alike who are on the front lines of raising youth."*

—Alex Craighead, MAT
Educator, Speaker, and Co-founder of Journeymen Institute

"SEL Muscle Mastery *is for anyone wishing to broaden relationship skills with young people, family, colleagues, and the larger community. Lori Woodley-Langendorff has effectively outlined what and how to strengthen our core communications and trust-building muscles. Every incoming teacher and expectant family/carer should be given a copy of this book!"*

—Justine Fischer
Family and Youth Engagement Advocate

"These all-too-familiar stories encourage educators, parents, and carers to notice the emotional tyranny we unnecessarily subject ourselves to. Lori Woodley-Langendorff's SEL Muscles empower readers with simple skills to choose and strategies to act, thus promoting harmony in our homes and classrooms. The author reassures us that although these muscles may not be easy to flex, it gets easier with time."

—Christina Fitzgerald
Director of Curriculum and Instruction,
Westside Union School District, California

"Lori Woodley-Langendorff's SEL Muscle Mastery *is an inspiring and actionable guide for educators and carer navigating the complexities of social-emotional learning. With relatable anecdotes, practical tools, and a focus on empowering both adults and young people, this book delivers on its promise to foster resilience, connection, and growth. Its emphasis on self-awareness and modeling positive behaviors makes it a transformative resource for anyone committed to creating trusted spaces where communities thrive. This is a must-read for those passionate about impactful education and personal growth."*

—Ronald Holt, DO, MA
University Psychiatrist, California

"This book provides a resource for adults to learn more about SEL and how this can impact how they approach a task or problem with their students. This is a much needed resource for any adult that is working with students. Modeling, teaching, and learning how to listen and respond is crucial as mental health concerns continue to rise in our young people. This resource would be a great addition to the work of our mental health wellness team. Equipping the adults with a clear understanding of their mental health and recognizing how we respond to student needs."

—Katina Keener
Associate Director of Student Services,
Gloucester County Public Schools, VA

"As a school counselor, I am profoundly inspired by Lori Woodley-Langendorff's unwavering dedication to empowering others through social-emotional learning. Her book, SEL Muscle Mastery, *introduces the transformative Notice Choose Act framework, which has significantly enhanced my ability to support students' emotional and social development. By treating SEL as a muscle to be strengthened, this guide provides practical strategies that have elevated my practice and deepened my connection with students. Lori's commitment to cultivating atmospheres where individuals recognize their inherent greatness and the interconnectedness of our life journeys makes this an invaluable resource for educators devoted to nurturing well-rounded individuals."*

—Cher Kretz, MS, PPS
School Counselor, TEDx Speaker,
Podcast Host of *The Focused Mindset*

"SEL Muscle Mastery *serves as a blueprint for developing and strengthening essential life skills—self-awareness, self-management, social awareness, relationship-building, and decision-making. The powerful concept of Notice Choose Act transforms us from passive bystanders into active difference-makers. Written in a user-friendly style, this book empowers educators and carers alike to foster meaningful relationships, personal growth, and lasting change. While SEL Muscles are not a new concept, Lori Woodley-Langendorff inspires readers to actively engage in strengthening what matters most: relationships."*

—Alma Lopez, MS, PPS
District School Counseling Coordinator
2021 California School Counselor of the Year
2022 National School Counselor of the Year

"SEL Muscle Mastery *is a transformative and essential guide for educators and carers seeking to build resilience and foster deep connections with students. Lori Woodley-Langendorff masterfully blends research-backed strategies with relatable storytelling, equipping readers with practical SEL tools that create trusted spaces for growth. This book is a must-read for anyone dedicated to supporting the well-being of young people while strengthening their emotional intelligence and leadership."*

—Homero M. Magaña, EdD
Tenure-Track Instructor and Fieldwork Coordinator,
Graduate Counselor Education Program,
California Lutheran University

"With over 20 years of experience teaching Grades 6–12, my success has been rooted in building positive relationships in a student-centered classroom. The ideas Lori Woodley-Langendorff shares in this book reinforce the work I was lucky enough to witness and learn from her as a colleague, and I found myself once again being reminded and reenergized by what I read. Veteran teachers and new teachers alike, along with other VIPs in students' lives, will find encouragement that well-being matters and can make all the difference in the way we are equipped to better our students' lives and educational experiences."

—Jill Magnante, MEd
High School English Teacher, California

"This book is a must-have for educators seeking to foster students' social-emotional growth while also nurturing their own well-being. Packed with practical strategies, it equips teachers to create supportive, empathetic learning environments without sacrificing self-care. SEL Muscle Mastery *is a powerful guide for balanced and sustainable SEL practice."*

—Marcy Melvin, MA
Behavioral Health Executive, Texas

"The author of SEL Muscle Mastery *feels like a trusted friend sitting down to share practical, powerful tools for communicating with heart and clarity. Through simple, relatable advice like using "I-statements," not taking things personally, and getting clear on what you need, it offers strategies anyone can apply in everyday life. Whether in a classroom, at home, or in any relationship, these tools—perfectly described as muscles to practice and strengthen—are thoughtfully presented in a way that's both easy to read and genuinely empowering."*

—Renee Nealon
Fourth/Fifth Grade Teacher,
Petaluma City Schools, CA

"This is a powerful and practical guide that helps you cultivate emotional intelligence through a blend of personal reflection and actionable strategies. Designed for both educators and parents, each chapter offers insightful exercises and creative prompts that allow you to make the content your own, fostering deeper connections and personal growth. Whether journaling, reflecting, or engaging with the material in another way, this book provides valuable tools to navigate everyday life with awareness and intention."

—Stephen Pietrolungo, EdD
Middle and High School Principal, Simi Valley, California

"Lori Woodley-Langendorff's SEL Muscle Mastery *offers a groundbreaking approach to building emotional intelligence and resilience. Through practical exercises and insightful strategies, it empowers readers to strengthen key social and emotional skills that are vital for success in both personal and professional settings. It's a must-read for anyone looking to enhance their emotional well-being and navigate life's challenges with confidence and empathy. This book is an invaluable resource for educators, parents, and individuals alike!"*

—Daniel Pratt
Teacher/Coach

"If you are looking for practical ways to create emotional resilience, look no further than SEL Muscle Mastery*. This is a masterful work with practical applications for anyone looking to help either themselves or others grow their emotional intelligence. Lori Woodley-Langendorff's work is based on practical experience as well as research and is easy to read and apply. Having personally observed her work with children over a long period of time, this book summarizes all that Lori has gleaned in those experiences as well as the work she has done with notable experts in this space. Reading it will give you a new perspective or will reinforce and extend what you are already thinking!"*

—Regina L. Rossall
Superintendent, CA

"SEL Muscle Mastery *is a book for anyone who works with children. Helping students develop SEL skills ensures our children flourish not only in the school setting, but also in life! Teaching children to notice, choose, and act at an early age helps them to be empathetic to those around them as well as reflective of their own impact."*

—Shannon Rossall-Bennett, EdD
Educator and Parent, California

"SEL Muscle Mastery *is a game-changer for educators, providing six powerful tools to build resilience, emotional intelligence, and authentic connection in schools and communities. This book goes beyond theory, offering practical strategies that transform classroom culture, deepen student engagement, and create lasting impact. By strengthening SEL educators, Lori empowers students with the confidence and skills they need to navigate life's challenges with resilience and purpose. This is a must-read for anyone committed to shaping the future of education.*

—Christopher Salem
Award Winning Author and Executive Coach

"The timing of SEL Muscle Mastery *is perfect: this book highlights the critical need for developing emotional intelligence and interpersonal skills, especially for educators and caregivers working with young people. In today's complex, fast-paced world, these "SEL muscles" seem increasingly important for building strong relationships and supporting healthy development. The framework is grounded in research and best practices, making it a credible approach. Additionally, the author's tone is warm, understanding, and invites the reader to be a partner in the process. This helps establish trust and credibility, making the guidance throughout the book feel more accessible and supportive."*

—Terri Serey
Assistant Principal,
Hacienda La Puente Unified, CA

"SEL Muscle Mastery *is an extraordinary resource for educators, parents, and caregivers who want to nurture resilience and empathy in young people. Lori's innovative strategies bridge the gap between emotional intelligence and happiness, offering practical tools that inspire lasting change. Her work is a beacon of hope for creating more compassionate schools and communities."*

—Marci Shimoff
#1 *NY Times* Bestselling
Author of Happy for No Reason and
Chicken Soup for the Woman's Soul

"SEL Muscle Mastery *offers a revolutionary and thought-provoking way to teach and learn, especially with the advancement of AI, the fastest-growing technology in human history. Lori Woodley-Langendroff's insights and practices are needed for human beings to live, think, and love."*

—Bettie Spruill
CEO, Ideal Coaching Global,
Transformational Leader and Writer

"SEL Muscle Mastery *is an essential tool kit for educators and caregivers alike. Through powerful messaging and relatable anecdotes, Lori Woodley-Langendorff equips readers with feasible ways to foster healthy relationships with children and adolescents. As an education researcher and a former special education teacher, I find this book particularly powerful because it encourages sustainable practices that may mitigate educator burnout and caregiver fatigue. Readers are guided with actionable steps to help them grow as individuals so they can better support others with various needs."*

—Alicia A. Stewart-Kitten, PhD
University of North Carolina at Charlotte

"With this book, Lori completely took me out of my comfort zone. She took me outside of the books with which I had been taught, the mentoring I had, and the lessons I learned while attending school. She made me grow me in ways that have made me a force to be reckoned with as a school counselor."

—Nicole Vitto
School Counselor,
Conejo Valley Unified School District, CA

"Lori Woodley-Langendorff's SEL Muscle Mastery *is an essential guide for educators, parents, and carers committed to shaping resilient, empathetic, and self-aware young people. Lori introduces the SEL Muscles—transformative tools like Quit Taking It Personally (QTIP) and Walk the Talk—offering a practical framework for navigating emotional challenges with clarity and compassion. Her engaging approach invites readers to rethink how they engage with young people, emphasizing connection, trust, and mutual growth. By integrating personal stories, actionable strategies, and the innovative Notice Choose Act framework, Lori equips readers to meet challenges with purpose and optimism. This book not only uplifts young lives but also rejuvenates the adults guiding them. It is a must-read for anyone striving to foster meaningful relationships and resiliency in our children and youth."*

—Loretta Whitson, EdD
Executive Director, California
Association of School Counselors

SEL Muscle Mastery

Six Tools for Building Resilience and Connection in Schools and Communities

Lori Woodley-Langendorff

Foreword by Pedro A, Noguera

CORWIN

FOR INFORMATION:

Corwin
A SAGE Company
2455 Teller Road
Thousand Oaks, California 91320
(800) 233-9936
www.corwin.com

SAGE Publications Ltd.
1 Oliver's Yard
55 City Road
London EC1Y 1SP
United Kingdom

SAGE Publications India Pvt. Ltd.
Unit No 323-333, Third Floor, F-Block
International Trade Tower Nehru Place
New Delhi 110 019
India

SAGE Publications Asia-Pacific Pte. Ltd.
18 Cross Street #10-10/11/12
China Square Central
Singapore 048423

Vice President and Editorial Director: Monica Eckman
Senior Publisher: Jessica Allan
Senior Content Development Editor: Mia Rodriguez
Project Editor: Amy Schroller
Copy Editor: Melinda Masson
Typesetter: C&M Digitals (P) Ltd.
Proofreader: Dennis Webb
Cover Designers: Paige Pelletier and Tanner Woodley
Marketing Manager: Olivia Bartlett

Printed and bound by CPI Group (UK) Ltd, Croydon, CR0 4YY

ISBN 978-1-0719-8023-1

This book is printed on acid-free paper.

25 26 27 28 29 10 9 8 7 6 5 4 3 2 1

Contents

MUSCLE #3: ASK VS. TELL

MUSCLE #4: STORYTELLING

MUSCLE #5: CURIOSITY

MUSCLE #6: WALK THE TALK

Foreword

It's taken a while, but policymakers finally seem to realize that hungry, sick, and mentally distressed children often do not do well in school. Most parents have known this for much longer, but unfortunately, the concerns of parents tend not to matter much in setting education policy in the United States. For too long, the social and emotional needs of children have been largely ignored as policymakers have pressured schools to generate higher levels of achievement. As policymakers have decried persistent disparities in achievement (the so-called achievement gap) and mediocre results when the United States is compared to other nations, too often they have failed to address the obvious fact that the kids with the greatest needs generally do the least well academically.

For a variety of reasons, it appears we are now ready for a new approach. In this book, Lori Woodley-Langendorff offers a practical guide to a new approach. In plain language she explains why helping adults to develop what she calls their social and emotional literacy—or "SEL Muscles"—is so important. Though their primary role is to address the educational needs of students, many educators now understand that they must also develop their capacity to respond to the social and emotional needs of students. Such skills create a classroom environment that is conducive to good teaching and learning. Students learn through relationships, and when relationships are strained or dysfunctional, it is often extremely difficult for teachers or school counselors to carry out their responsibilities.

The question is this: How should educators acquire and cultivate these essential skills? Though parents often know more about their children, they will benefit from the development of these skills, or "muscles" as the author describes them, that are essential for helping children develop into healthy, balanced adults.

Woodley-Langendorff reminds us that during the height of the COVID-19 pandemic, such skills became as important as knowing how to master the technology required to teach virtually. We knew that large numbers of students were struggling with stress and fear caused by the uncertainty of the pandemic and with depression often related to prolonged isolation. The author and her colleagues created a groundbreaking film, *A Trusted Space: Redirecting Grief to Growth*, to draw attention to these issues. The film had a virtual reach across all 50 states and 27 countries, reaching tens of thousands of educators who were desperately trying to navigate the effects of quarantine and the pandemic. The documentary proved to be a critical affirmation of the work many educators were doing—providing comfort to students in need even though many had no formal training as counselors.

Recognizing the need to broaden the public's understanding of the widespread mental health challenges facing many children, and in some cases educators, Woodley-Langendorff designed the *Building Trusted Spaces in Five Days* curriculum so that educators had access to the skills and strategies needed to provide their students with support in social, emotional, and mental health.

Woodley-Langendorff has now written this book to serve as another resource for educators. Again, it comes at a critical time. Though schools have been back open for over three years, many continue to face alarming challenges related to problematic behavior (including fights and drug use), a variety of persistent mental health issues, and a noted increase in chronic absenteeism. The prevalence of these issues has made it difficult for schools to focus exclusively on teaching and learning, and many are now more open to developing their SEL Muscles.

Throughout the United States, there is growing interest in the concept and practice of wellness. Wellness is now being embraced by a number of schools to respond holistically to the needs of students. Instead of reacting after an incident or crisis, the wellness approach calls for a preventive strategy to promote wellness and health outcomes. For example, wellness advocates encourage us to treat food as a form of medicine because good nutrition is essential for health and well-being. Similarly, wellness advocates encourage us to treat exercise as a means of preventing illness, to get enough sleep and rest to prevent fatigue and burnout, and to have regular access to play and recreation to promote joy and healthy relationships.

In a similar vein, Woodley-Langendorff's new book encourages readers to develop their SEL Muscles because such capacities and skills are critical to the wellness and well-being of students. Such skills are also vital for educators, parents, and carers. She reminds us that healthy relationships can't be taken for granted; they don't typically emerge on their own. Rather, the development of healthy relationships and social skills in kids requires intentional development, attention, and participation if we are to create nurturing and supportive communities. By developing our SEL Muscles, we can create school communities where every member—students, families, and staff—experiences a sense of belonging, care, and trust.

SEL Muscles are needed because we are in the midst of a "crisis of connection" (NYU Press, 2014). In 2014, I coauthored a book on this topic with my colleagues Niobe Way, Alisha Ali, and Carol Gilligan, documenting how loneliness and social isolation were growing, reinforced by the myth of "rugged individualism." Together, these trends have produced an empathy gap and reinforced the social fragmentation that makes it increasingly difficult for our society to tackle a variety of social ills including a dramatic rise in what sociologists refer to as "deaths of despair"—rising suicide rates, overdose deaths caused by substance abuse, and so on.

In the pages ahead, Lori Woodley-Langendorff shows us how to build our SEL Muscles to counter the crisis of connection by constructing strong, nurturing communities in our schools. This book is timely, the strategies the author provides are practical, and the skills she encourages us to develop will make our schools better places for all.

Pedro A. Noguera, PhD
Emery Stoops and Joyce King Stoops Dean
Rossier School of Education
University of Southern California

Preface

For decades I have been a school counselor, a mom, a partner, and a hard-working, deeply empathic woman who has pressed her introverted nature to the very edges of comfort. I have learned most of my important life lessons from those I care most about, starting with my children and extended family, and through service-oriented work starting at age 18 in a domestic violence shelter.

I thought I had most of it figured out and under control when I became a school counselor, a wife, and a mom in my mid-20s.

LITTLE DID I KNOW HOW MUCH I HAD YET TO LEARN!

The biggest lesson I recognized and am reminded of still today is that I am a work in progress, an ever-evolving, perfectly imperfect, and uniquely individual human. I seek to understand and grow even when I seem to be slipping backwards. I see myself in every other human's eye, and I realize that we are more alike than different and that we are all doing the best we can with what we know in any given moment. I learned compassion for myself in my service to others. I learned that what I could see in others I deserved to see in myself.

For years I was relentless on myself, a champion of others while not seeing or celebrating *me*. I could not see the impact of this, on myself or on others who cared deeply for me. The need to constantly improve bled out into my actions, my words, and my requirements for perfection, which inherently is an impossible task and untenable responsibility. I lived to prove rather than demonstrate my value. Learning to be self-accepting and vulnerable were skills that changed my life, and over time I began to repair compromised relationships.

What I recognized over years in education is that educators and parents or carers often are in a similar situation, where they are so focused outward that the person in the mirror is blurry and unrecognizable. In my work, I cultivate atmospheres where audiences feel the power of their greatness, a blend of outward and inward focus, developing traits that can up-level lives without dictating the path. As I evolved my own desired outcomes and recognized the positive impact I have on others, I realized that one cannot exist without the other: My life journey influences yours, and your life journey influences mine. It is the way in which we choose to influence and receive or repel influence, both within and outside of ourselves, that creates our personal joy and well-being. Identifying how to do this with wisdom and purpose is the work.

The SEL Muscles™ were not always called such. I wrote and facilitated trainings that focused on similar skills, and I worked hard to live what I taught. It was bumpy for sure, but even small steps forward count as forward progress! Then, on June 3, 2020, in the middle of a global pandemic, I received a text that added new direction to my life's work.

"Please, get that new producer friend of yours, and let's make a film on trauma. Our teachers are going to need to understand it more than ever, and if they have to pay to attend a workshop, they will not be able to afford it."

—Christina Fitzgerald

Director of Curriculum and Instruction, Westside Union School District, California

---

Everyone was pivoting that summer—families and education ecosystems—and my organization was no different. My nervous system was in a daily battle of fight, flight, or freeze, and suddenly there was a direction. Without any qualms I sent out the call, and within two days we had a commitment from Emmy Award–winning documentary film producer Karin Gornick and a small but mighty film crew, Skerritt Creative, to create what would, two and a half months later, become an expert-driven and award-winning film, *A Trusted Space: Redirecting Grief to Growth*, accompanied with a research-based curriculum, *Building Trusted Spaces in Five Days*.

It was a whirlwind summer, doing two huge projects during the pandemic, each of which would typically take about nine months. Bringing together decades of personal and professional work and learning and the urgency of the moment, the SEL Muscles came to life.

Everyone was talking about how we were going to need more from our educators to support our young people, but what about the educators and parents themselves—what would they need to reach a place where they could meet the needs of their young people? This question was a catalyst for the SEL Muscles.

By the time the film and curriculum were released in September 2020, the project was embraced by neuroscientists at the University of Southern California and researchers at the Hackett Center for Mental Health in Texas, to name just a couple. Viewers accessed the film from all 50 states, 27 countries, and networks such as PBS, and education organizations such as the American Federation of Teachers put it on their educator resource platforms. Our little nonprofit simply wanted to support the education system and never could have guessed the impact we would have.

Jump forward four years, and the five SEL Muscles became six SEL Muscles, while *A Trusted Space*, born as one film, became more than 40. As films dropped, curriculum expanded, and need continued to grow, SEL Muscles and Building Trusted Spaces trainings took off across the country.

Finally, it was time for the book.

Welcome!

Key Words, Phrases, and Ideas

Each of us responds differently to various words and approaches, and my hope is to offer you meaningful content that meets you right where you are. I invite you to consider the content in this book and, if the words, phrases, and approaches are not a fit but the content is, change them to something that resonates with you.

Acknowledgment: There are as many different ideas, beliefs, mindsets, cultural identifications, and lived experiences as there are humans on the planet. There is incredible alchemy in the way each person's independent worldview feeds into the collective. While I make every effort to find examples and approaches that will reach a wide range of people, I know I will miss addressing the experience of every person. If you do not see your specific circumstances reflected, it is my hope that you can find relatability and insights through the situations of others.

Educators: If you serve students in the education ecosystem, regardless of role, I consider you an educator. Whether you are in the classroom, supervising the playground, driving a bus, running a wellness center, or greeting students and parents in the front office, you are influencing our young people and their families, and hence you are an educator. The SEL Muscles are for all of you, and they will serve you well.

Parents, Carers, and Families: Throughout the book I refer to adults at home as parents and carers. This group of people includes moms, dads, aunties, uncles, grandparents, foster parents, friends, and all other titles not listed who are raising our young people. There is no "one look" or "one title" for families, and all who are raising children fall into the title of parent or carer for this book.

Community: If you are not a parent/carer or an educator, you are likely still part of a community that cares about the future of our young people while also trying to balance personal wellness with the overwhelm and worry that life can create. If you are looking to experience more ease, peace of mind, and happiness, this book is a resource for you too.

Serve vs. Save: It is my belief that our role is to serve our young people in ways that help them develop skills to take on their social, emotional, mental, and academic well-being. We need to be modeling this for them while believing in their ability to learn and apply the skills themselves. If we save them from paving their way through all the terrains—easy, fun, hard, sad—we are not preparing them for a future they can manage and thrive in regardless of circumstance. You will recognize that the SEL Muscles are intended to serve, not save, starting with ourselves.

Social-Emotional Literacy (SEL), often known as social-emotional learning and emotional intelligence, includes skills such as teamwork, communication, decision-making, independent thinking, and leadership. Throughout this book I will be using the acronym SEL. I prefer to think of it as skills to become *literate* in, like reading or mathematics. They are skills that elevate one's ability to effectively navigate productive lives, with resilience and care, regardless of present and past circumstances. These skills support us through painful times and allow us to enjoy times of ease and success. It is my ultimate hope that one day SEL will become as important to develop and measure as all the other "academic" focuses our current education model prioritizes.

Triggered vs. Upset: At this point the word *triggered* is becoming part of mainstream vernacular and consciousness. We can all see people, places, memories, associations, and things that trigger us. In some cases they are minor, while in other cases they can feel almost impossible to not react to, at times evoking an actual trauma response. You will notice that I use terms such as *upset* interchangeably with *trigger* and their meaning is the same.

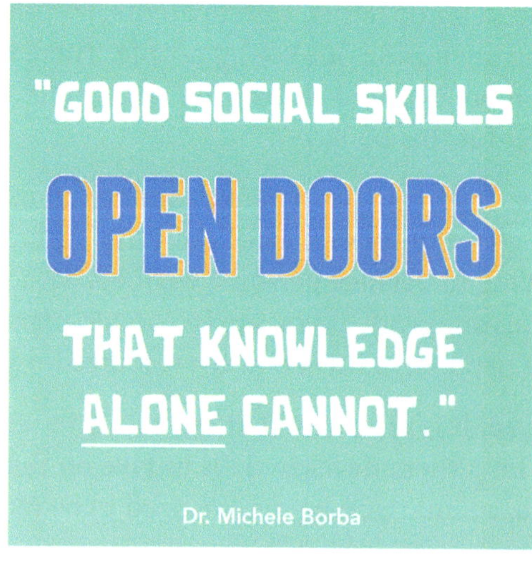

Purpose and Research

EVIDENCE OF EFFECTIVENESS

As mentioned in the preface, the original five SEL Muscles were developed over the summer of 2020 as a component of the *Building Trusted Spaces in Five Days* curriculum and in tandem with the production of the film *A Trusted Space: Redirecting Grief to Growth*. Both the curriculum, including the SEL Muscles, and the film, along with subsequent films in the series, were developed using evidence-informed and research-based practices and concepts. Additionally, in our commitment to provide meaningful and freely accessible resources to educators, we had the good fortune to partner with three nationally recognized clinical teams. These partners were Meadows Mental Health Policy Institute (MMHPI), the Hackett Center for Mental Health (HCMH), both based in Texas, and the University of Southern California (USC) Rossier School of Education.

Overseeing the clinical endorsement from MMHPI and the HCMH were the following professionals:

- Gary Blau, PhD, Executive Director
- Gwenn Blau, MA, Chief of Staff
- Jennifer Gonzalez, PhD, Senior Director of Population Health
- Marcy Melvin, MA, LPC, Senior Director of Health Equity Strategy
- Linda Rodriguez, EdD, Senior Director for School Behavioral Health
- Patrick Tennant, PhD, Project Manager

Clinical partners at USC Rossier included the following:

- Alan Arkatov, Katzman/Ernst Chair in Educational Entrepreneurship, Technology, and Innovation
- Rebecca Gotlieb, PhD, USC Provost's Research and Teaching Fellow
- Mary Helen Immordino-Yang, EdD, Neuroscientist, Human Development Psychologist

The clinical partners were responsible for reviewing and assessing the curriculum in its entirety. The SEL Muscles became highlighted as a critical element contributing to the program's qualitative and quantitative success. Recognized by both teams for their emphasis on enhancing educators' social-emotional literacy skills, the SEL Muscles play a pivotal role in fostering healthy relationships. These connections are vital for supporting students' emotional health and academic achievement while simultaneously promoting the well-being of educators and carers.

The six SEL Muscles are high-level communication skills that are as much about our impact on ourselves as they are about our impact on others. Independently, some of the SEL Muscles are skills often identified as key to having healthy relationships, engaging in positive and courageous leadership, and developing resilience while balancing personal and professional desires and needs. Authors and researchers who speak to these skills each come from their own worldview and present to the audience they serve.

My passion is for educators and the young scholars and families they serve, and in defining the SEL Muscles it was clear that developed, strengthened, and flexed together these skills could be game-changing both personally and across educational settings (a top priority). I have sought out and received anonymous observations from SEL Muscle users and received several streams of feedback that point to evidence of the skills' efficacy. These include the clinical endorsement of the aforementioned esteemed partners, the body of research pointing to the urgent need to elevate teacher wellness, and the unbiased feedback we've received from early SEL Muscle trainings and prepublished reviews of the book. Through this feedback, I received overwhelming commentary that the SEL Muscles, whether standing alone or as a part of our Building Trusted Spaces or other trainings, serve as powerful tools to support educators and carers facing unprecedented times.

Whether trying to get our kids off their devices and ready for a good night's sleep or trying to engage them in caring about their own educational development, navigating growing emotional turmoil is often beyond our reliable skill set. The SEL Muscles are a positive place to start.

How to Use This Book

This book is intended to be your working guide—A Trusted Space® in a book, a place where you not only feel seen and heard but experience understanding and value while simultaneously equipping yourself with tools that are tangible and practical to your everyday life. Within each chapter you will find an introduction to one of the SEL Muscles as well as a section dedicated to educators and a section for parents and carers.

Each chapter ends with summary of chapter highlights and a reflection opportunity that I invite you to engage with in whatever way feels right to you. Journal, wonder and ponder, talk to a friend, process into a voice recording, doodle or create interpretive art, or dance it out. Do whatever works best for you to internalize the material and make it your own.

Acknowledgments

AUTHOR'S ACKNOWLEDGMENTS

To my best friend and husband, Dave, who kept me going—you're my greatest champion who also kept me nourished (literally) while patiently waiting countless hours for me to be "done," which of course never happened but you kept bringing meals, shoulder rubs, tea, and roses from the garden anyways.

To Tanner and Shailene, the two most caring, compassionate humans who I get to call my kids, my muses, my greatest pride, and my dearest teachers. Tanner, your dedication to me, the work we do, and ultimately the impact we make in the world has inspired me to keep going no matter how daunting the times. Your endless talent, patience, and insights helped make *SEL Muscle Mastery* lift off pages and settle into hearts. Shailene, my beautifully talented, courageous, and powerful girl who decided with her mama in 2010 to start All It Takes, your commitment to me ultimately made this book possible, and it would not be a reality without your open-hearted generosity and commitment to a better world. I am blessed to share this milestone with you both.

To Jessica Allan, Corwin's visionary publisher who gave this first-time author a chance. You have been a dream to work with, a believer who navigated all my questions with understanding and patience—always rooting me on while at the same time letting me be. To the instrumental extended Corwin/Sage team who have been committed and patient teachers—Mia Rodriguez (content development editor), Olivia Bartlett (marketing), Erica Capogreco (sales), Amy Schroller (project editor), and all those behind the scenes who I have not yet met—it takes a village to raise a child, and so goes for publishing a book! It has been reassuring knowing I am in such expert hands.

To Melinda Masson, copy editor extraordinaire. I didn't know what to expect when we hit the copyediting stage, and your ease and expertise settled my anxiety and organized not just the process but my brain in the process. *SEL Muscle Mastery* is better because of you!

To Jasmine Carey, whose gifted talent and collaborative support helped make the SEL Muscles come alive—what a ride! I'm grateful to have been on it with you.

To Paige Pelletier, Tanner Woodley, Seamus McLean, and Seppi Dabringer, your artistic talent is nothing less than brilliant. Thank you for giving this project its own unique look and feel—it is stunning.

To Pedro Noguera, whose inspiring foreword calls on each of us to be undeterred in our service to our young people and our education system, I am happy to share that mindset with you. I have such gratitude for your tireless work and for contributing your expertise to this project.

To the amazing team of creators and experts behind the original, *A Trusted Space*, which is why the SEL Muscles developed (2020): Chris Fitzgerald, Karin Gornick, Jules Ho, Alan Arkatov, Pedro Noguera, Mary Helen Immordino Yang, Linda Darling-Hammond, Marcy Melvin, and Pamela Cantor. And to the countless voices from the trenches—educators, parents, and young people who shared your stories: You are my why.

To Team All It Takes—current and past—what we do and have done is changing and saving lives. I could not be more grateful for the contributions of each of you. And for those who were sprinting along beside me on this book-writing journey, Tanner, Paige, Rikke, Seamus, Wendy, Cortney, Jules, Paul, Dave, Karin, and Justine, you get to catch your breath now too!

To my early readers and reviewers, even before the book was in a final form you took precious time to review it, to send thoughts and guidance. Your insights made the final version stronger and more relatable. Your endorsements are proudly shared within this book—thank you.

Finally, to my angels, the ones who believe in me no matter what: Adriane, Andy, Cindy, Cortney, Dave, David, Derek, Jill, John, Joy, Jules, Justine, Karin, Lisa, Loretta, Marcy, Rikke, Roger, Shai, Stacy, Tanner, Theresa, Wendy, and my mama, Diane—the original angel.

PUBLISHER'S ACKNOWLEDGMENTS

Corwin gratefully acknowledges the contributions of the following reviewers:

Elizabeth Álvarez
Superintendent
Forest Park D91
Forest Park, Illinois

Melissa A. Campbell
K–5 Mathematics Specialist
University of Alabama in Huntsville Alabama Math, Science, and Technology Initiative (UAH AMSTI)
Huntsville, Alabama

Katina Keener
Associate Director of Student Services
Gloucester County Public Schools
Gloucester, Virginia

John Mahoney
National Teachers Hall of Fame

Renee Nealon
Fourth- and Fifth-Grade Teacher
Petaluma City Schools
Petaluma, California

Terri Serey
Assistant Principal
Hacienda La Puente Unified
Hacienda Heights, California

About the Author

CEO and founder of All It Takes®, **Lori Woodley-Langendorff, MS, PPS,** is an experiential keynote speaker, trainer, and author supporting youth and those who serve them to develop critical social-emotional literacy skills that empower them to successfully navigate their lives and support their communities through both joyful and trying times. A mother of two grown children, Lori has a combined 30+ years working as a school counselor, consultant, curriculum developer, and most recently author, creator, producer, and featured expert of the free-to-access award-winning film and curriculum series *A Trusted Space*. Additional productions include the California Association of School Counselors' *Heartbeat* video and the national public service announcement *This Is a Trusted Space*, which aired throughout 2024 to an audience of over 1.5 billion.

Professional publications include the following:

A Trusted Space: Redirecting Grief to Growth, 2020; *A Trusted Space* film series, 2023—featured expert and producer
www.allittakes.org/atrustedspace

Building Trusted Spaces in Five Days curriculum, 2020—author
https://www.allittakes.org/atrustedspace/redirectinggrieftogrowth

Leadership Development Through Physical Education (LDTPE), 2015, 2024 (version 1.4)—author
www.allittakes.org/ldtpe

Shine Your Light, 2017—featured author
www.amazon.com/Shine-Your-Light-Practices-Extraordinary/dp/168350545X

Introduction

THE POWER OF SEL MUSCLES IN OUR LIVES

Each of us walks a unique path shaped by the relationships, communities, and experiences that make up our lives. These communities—families, friendships, classrooms, workplaces, and social groups—form the backdrop to our personal and collective growth. To every interaction, we bring ourselves—our thoughts, beliefs, and emotions—and these interactions create ripples that reach far beyond us, influencing everyone we encounter.

In this book, I invite you to consider "community" expansively, to include any group of people bound together through shared experiences. This includes the familiar spaces we inhabit: family dinners, classroom discussions, team meetings, work environments, team sports, and social gatherings. Within each of these communities, we share responsibility for shaping the culture and norms and supporting one another's growth. At times, these relationships are sources of comfort and joy; at others, they bring challenges that require patience, understanding, and self-awareness.

Navigating this balance between individual growth and collective responsibility can be challenging, particularly for those of us in caregiving or educational roles. As parents, educators, carers, and mentors, we hold a unique responsibility: to guide young people toward healthy, resilient, and fulfilling adulthoods. We seek to support their growth, not only in the face of success but also through challenges and setbacks. But this role can be difficult, even overwhelming. The emotional ups and downs of guiding young people can lead to exhaustion and frustration. We may find ourselves at a loss, wondering if we're making the difference we hope to, or questioning our ability to keep going.

> **"Thank you. I am a different person today than I was yesterday."**
>
> **—Parent participant in the All It Takes Parent–Educator Leadership Training, October 2024**

These words capture the transformative potential of embracing a new approach to our interactions with young people, with all people actually. The quote reflects the core purpose of this book: to provide a set of tools, the SEL Muscles, that help us become not only effective guides but also more fulfilled, resilient, and empowered individuals. The SEL Muscles were created to bridge the gap between our intentions and the realities we encounter, supporting us in engaging with young people from a place of calm, compassion, and clarity. They're not about quick fixes but about developing lasting skills that bring joy and renewed purpose to our roles and our lives in general.

WHY SEL MUSCLES?

When we think of muscles, we typically associate an image of physical muscles—that is, biceps, abs, quads, and so on that each of us has and that are in a varied state of condition and strength. We know that they get stronger when we intentionally work on them, and they get weaker when we don't pay enough attention to them. Some of us have naturally strong muscles, and others find it frustrating that we have to work twice as hard to make any headway at all. I see the SEL Muscles in the same way: as mental muscles that need to be exercised to become stronger, more conditioned, and more flexible, making us socially, emotionally, and mentally healthier people in happier relationships.

For a physical workout, if you're stepping into a gym for the first time ever, it's not a good idea to go directly to the heavy weightlifting area. In fact, doing so may result in a painful outcome that causes you to give up on the process altogether. A more manageable and healthy approach would be to start small and begin building your muscles, navigating setbacks but not needing to retreat completely because you broke your body. Building and flexing your SEL Muscles is the same: Start gently with the ones that are least familiar and the greatest challenge, give them a try, assess your progress, and step back into the workout. I promise that you will get stronger and you will experience greater ease and joy with every authentic flex of each SEL Muscle.

The purpose of the SEL Muscles is to offer practical, effective tools that provide relief, optimism, and a sense of agency for those supporting young people's development. Whether in a classroom, at home, or in a broader mentoring role, the SEL Muscles empower us to meet the evolving needs of the next generation with empathy and skill. Each SEL Muscle offers a way to approach challenges that honors both our own well-being and theirs. Even broader, it honors the well-being of all of us, from homes, to schools, to corporate boardrooms. Every one of us deserves to feel the power of the SEL Muscles!

Each SEL Muscle is designed to be accessible, powerful, and relevant, equipping us with the tools needed to build strong connections, foster resilience, and maintain clarity and calm in the face of difficult situations. While the SEL Muscles don't eliminate challenges, they allow us to navigate them with purpose and optimism. We cannot control every aspect of our relationships, but we can control how we choose to engage, respond, and grow, no matter who the other people are, young or older.

This book is organized into sections tailored specifically for educators and carers, acknowledging the unique demands of each role. Educators work within structured environments, balancing diverse personalities in a classroom and meeting the expectations of educational systems. Parents and carers, by contrast, encounter different challenges in the home, often shaped by emotional ties, family history, and enduring dynamics. These differences matter, and this book addresses the nuances of each setting, providing role-specific guidance that maximizes the effectiveness of each SEL Muscle.

While supporting young people's growth and resilience, adults who serve them can also develop a sense of ease, joy, and fulfillment in their roles. The SEL Muscles provide tools that nurture positive outcomes in young people and create environments where adults feel compelled to be aware of

> **"I want my teachers not only to notice when I'm struggling, but to act on it and get me the help I need."**
>
> - Student

their wellness while being more grounded and empowered. By working collaboratively and finding common ground, parents, carers, and educators can foster a balanced approach that reduces stress, builds trust, and encourages shared success. This sense of connection and purpose uplifts entire communities, allowing adults and young people alike to thrive in spaces filled with understanding, support, and mutual respect.

THE SEL MUSCLES

At the heart of this book are six core SEL Muscles.

Each SEL Muscle has a specific function, but they are designed to work together, creating an emotionally intelligent tool kit for effective communication, expanded self-awareness, and collaborative problem-solving, to name a few. These SEL Muscles support us in building and maintaining relationships that are grounded in empathy, respect, and resilience.

Here's a brief look at each SEL Muscle and its purpose in this book:

1. **Quit Taking It Personally (QTIP):** Muscle #1 is about resisting the tendency to internalize the actions and words of others. Often, when people express frustration, anger, or indifference, it has more to do with their own experiences than with us. QTIP encourages us to give them the benefit of the doubt, allowing us to respond from a place of calm rather than defensiveness.

2. **The Power of "I":** Muscle #2 centers on using "I" statements, which take ownership of our feelings and needs. This SEL Muscle is about creating a respectful dialogue by focusing on our own experiences rather than assigning blame or judgment. By using "I" statements, we prevent unnecessary defensiveness and model self-awareness.

3. **Ask vs. Tell:** Muscle #3 encourages us to shift from complaint-driven dialogue to constructive problem-solving. Instead of venting frustrations, we focus on understanding needs and finding solutions. Recognizing what we need and asking questions rather than making demands helps us foster a sense of collaboration and responsibility in our interactions.

4. **Storytelling:** Muscle #4 is a powerful way to build trust and connection. Rather than teaching a lesson or imparting advice, storytelling allows us to share our own experiences in a way that invites others to see themselves in our stories. This SEL Muscle strengthens empathy and emotional connection, making it easier to navigate difficult situations and conversations.

5. **Curiosity:** Muscle #5 replaces judgment with inquiry, giving us the space to explore situations with openness. This SEL Muscle helps us respond to tension and resistance with understanding rather than reaction, allowing us to hold space for the experience of others without compromising our own values.

6. **Walk the Talk:** Muscle #6 is about modeling the values we encourage in young people. It means embodying integrity, accountability, and resilience. This SEL Muscle is one of the most challenging, as it requires us to live out the lessons we hope to teach, showing young people what it looks like to embrace imperfection and personal growth. Like all the SEL Muscles, this one also supports our credibility and fulfilment with all our relationships.

EDUCATORS: HOW SEL MUSCLES TRANSFORM THE CLASSROOM

For educators, the SEL Muscles offer a practical framework for managing classroom dynamics and finding personal fulfillment, all while supporting the whole child. In recent years, educators have faced growing challenges that require advanced skill sets to meet the evolving needs of our young people while also meeting academic standards. This environment requires educators to act as teachers, relationship-builders, and role models, often without adequate training and support.

The SEL Muscles can make a significant difference in this context, helping educators manage their own stress while fostering a positive classroom culture. For example, QTIP helps teachers remain calm when faced with student outbursts, preventing escalation and demonstrating emotional regulation. Similarly, the Power of "I" allows teachers to address behavioral issues without assigning blame, reducing defensiveness and encouraging students to reflect on their actions.

The benefits of the SEL Muscles extend beyond behavior management. When educators use Ask vs. Tell, they invite students to take ownership of their actions and learning, creating a collaborative environment where students feel respected and involved. Storytelling allows teachers to connect with students on a personal level, sharing experiences that build trust and empathy. Walk the Talk is particularly important for educators, as students are quick to notice inconsistencies between what adults say and do. By modeling the behaviors they value, educators build credibility and set an example that students are more likely to follow.

PARENTS AND CARERS: HOW SEL MUSCLES STRENGTHEN FAMILY RELATIONSHIPS

For parents and carers, the SEL Muscles offer a framework for building strong, trusting relationships with young people. Family life brings unique challenges, shaped by deep emotional ties, shared history, and the ongoing demands of daily life. Unlike educators, parents are not only guides but also companions in young people's lives, witnessing both their highs and their lows.

The SEL Muscles provide tools for managing these complexities with compassion and consistency.

> At home, **QTIP** helps parents avoid taking hurtful words or challenging behavior personally, allowing them to respond with empathy rather than defensiveness. This can be especially important during adolescence, when young people often test boundaries and express frustration in ways that can feel personal.

The Power of "I" enables parents to communicate their feelings without assigning blame, creating space for open dialogue. Instead of saying, "You never listen to me," a parent might say, "I feel unheard when we talk about this." This shift reduces tension and models accountability, helping young people understand the impact of their actions.

Ask vs. Tell transforms family dynamics by shifting from complaint-driven dialogue to collaborative problem-solving. By understanding our needs that delve into collaborative problem-solving rather than complaining about what is not done, parents encourage young people to take responsibility for their well-being and actions and contribute to solutions. For instance, instead of saying, "You need to keep your room clean," a parent might note: "I need for our home to be a healthy environment. This includes your room. What do you think would help you keep your room cleaner and more organized?"

Storytelling is equally powerful in the family setting. By sharing personal stories of challenge, fear, or joy, parents create a trusted space for young people to express themselves without fear of judgment. Rather than focusing on the lesson or moral of the story, storytelling emphasizes emotional connection and shared experience. For example, a parent might share an experience of feeling scared in a new situation, focusing on how it felt rather than what happened or how they "fixed it." This shift from "here's what I learned" to "this is what I felt" helps young people feel understood and valued, knowing that they're not alone in their experiences. Storytelling, in this way, fosters understanding and trust, allowing for a deeper relationship that can weather the challenges of family life.

It's clear that these tools are not only practical; they're transformative. They're designed to support those of us who guide, teach, and nurture young people by enhancing our ability to connect, communicate, and grow with them and each other.

The SEL Muscles remind us that progress, not perfection, is the goal. Just as with physical muscles, the SEL Muscles require consistent, mindful use and a willingness to embrace growth over time. The strength of each SEL Muscle comes from regular practice, and the benefits are cumulative: greater ease, deeper relationships, and a sense of purpose and fulfillment in our work and families.

Throughout this book, you'll find exercises, stories, and examples tailored to both educators and carers. Each chapter will explore a specific SEL Muscle, offering insights and strategies for flexing it in ways that resonate with your unique role, whether that's in the classroom, at home, or in the community. You'll also find the Notice Choose Act® framework integrated into each SEL Muscle's exploration, providing a structured way to observe your responses, make intentional choices, and act in ways that support positive outcomes for you.

The journey you're embarking on is as much about self-discovery as it is about serving young people.

By strengthening these SEL Muscles, you're investing not only in young people's well-being but also in your own. Together, these tools allow you to build a life where connection, empathy, and resilience flourish—a life where you can meet challenges with confidence and joy, knowing that your actions truly matter.

As we move forward, let's embrace the opportunity to grow, flexing each SEL Muscle with purpose and patience. Whether in times of ease or challenge, the SEL Muscles offer a path toward greater understanding, collaboration, and fulfillment.

So, take a deep breath, roll up your sleeves, and get ready to dive in. Let's start building the foundation for a life of purpose, joy, and connection, one SEL Muscle at a time.

NOTICE.CHOOSE.ACT.®

Another way to think about it: **Awareness. Intention. Results.**

It's easy to take in new ideas—whether through reading or listening—and feel a spark of inspiration, nodding along and thinking, "Yes, that's exactly what I need!" In those moments, it's tempting to believe that this fresh insight will transform our lives. But once we're back in the flow of everyday routines, that spark fades, and the idea quietly retreats to the background. Occasionally, it whispers, "You should give it a try," or nags, "You know things would be better if you were doing that." Yet without action, these whispers can lead to a sense of frustration, even self-doubt, slowly chipping away at our confidence and sense of achievement.

After years of working with students and families, I've seen first-hand the importance of having instructions that go beyond "Do this" or "Don't do that." Real change—especially in behaviors and attitudes—requires more than just orders or suggestions. Telling middle school students or siblings to "be nice" seldom reshapes their actions or the way they treat each other. ***True transformation comes not from commands but from practical tools and intentional practice***.

NOTICE CHOOSE ACT: THE FRAMEWORK TO ACHIEVE SEL MUSCLE MASTERY

This same principle applies to the SEL Muscles. You might feel a pull to try flexing one of them, but in the heat of a challenging moment—when a young person is testing your limits or a colleague has dismissed your ideas—having the knowledge alone won't necessarily help you access it. That's where Notice Choose Act (NCA) comes into play. This framework helps you develop awareness of the impact that using, or not using, a particular SEL Muscle has on both yourself and those around you. With this awareness comes a powerful sense of agency, allowing you to shift from autopilot reactions to intentional responses, creating outcomes that reflect the values you aim to bring to each interaction. The NCA framework is a tool for problem-solving and productive decision-making, and it can transform how you approach challenging situations and relationships with yourself and others.

TRY THIS to understand the concept of moving from autopilot to intentional action.

1. Cross your arms. (Yes, it's that simple.)

   Notice and reflect:

   - Was that hard?
   - Did you have to think about it?
   - What did it take to do it?

2. Uncross your arms and shake them out. Then cross them backwards (put the opposite arm on top).

   Notice and reflect:

   - Was that hard? (Maybe awkward.)
   - Did you have to think about it? (Usually, yes.)
   - What did it take to do it? (Intention, thinking, and purposeful action.)

Change can be awkward, unsettling, and sometimes challenging. But it usually only takes remembering to cross backwards to keep us moving forward!

NOTICE.

As you dive deeper into each of the SEL Muscles, you will notice that I use the word *notice* often. Noticing is the practice of becoming aware. Without the Notice step, nothing really ever changes. Nothing gets invented, improved, corrected, fixed, or even celebrated. It may seem a simple concept, but in a world where many folks are on autopilot most of the time, the purposeful act of noticing creates epiphanies that allow openings for change.

There are three categories where noticing happens:

1. **Ourselves**
   - What do we notice about ourselves? What are we doing or experiencing?
   - How are we feeling? What are our behaviors?
2. **Others**
   - What do we notice about others? How are they feeling and acting?
   - What do they need? How do they influence us and others?

3. **Environment**
    - What is our footprint?
    - What does the environment need to be safer and healthier for all? (This can be both the environment we interact with and ecosystems at large.)

In each of the following chapters you will have the opportunity to explore what you notice about the SEL Muscle and how it plays a role in the outcomes you experience. I invite you to follow the reflection guide to open your awareness beyond what might lie on the surface and uncover what you feel and the behaviors that follow those feelings. Only in this awareness can you purposely identify what you are currently experiencing and determine what you might want instead.

Educator Examples

"I notice that I feel ineffective teaching almost every day. I notice I spend more time redirecting student behavior than delivering a fun and engaging lesson that I planned."

"I feel disappointed, defeated, unsupported, helpless, angry, and exhausted."

"My behaviors, words, and attitudes are cranky, isolating, impatient, and snappy."

Parent Examples

"I notice that every evening our home is chaotic as we work to get homework, dinner, showers, and bedtime done."

"I feel unhappy, frustrated, unsupported, angry, and overwhelmed."

"My behaviors, words, and attitudes are short, critical, aggressive, dismissive, and withdrawn."

CHOOSE.

Once we identify clearly what we are noticing, how we feel and behave, we can articulate what we want instead, if anything. If we like what we are aware of, we can keep on the same path.

Alternatively, if what we notice does not bring us personal or professional joy, ease, satisfaction, reasons to celebrate, and so on, then we can purposely choose something else.

The Choose step is a purposeful consideration of options that define what we desire rather than what we have. Using the examples in Notice, here is how Choose might look:

Educator Examples

"I choose to be successful in teaching my carefully planned, thoughtful, and fun lessons."

"I feel successful, connected, motivated, energized, productive, and creative."

"My behaviors, words, and attitudes are welcoming, considerate, curious, patient, and caring."

Parent Examples

"I choose an easy, fun, and connected evening with my family."

"I feel calm, happy, effective, valued, and respected."

"My behaviors, words, and attitudes are fun, helpful, connected, accepting, and engaged."

When comparing what each of these examples started as in Notice with where they got to in Choose, which one would you want to live in? If you created the atmosphere in Choose, would it serve you and your well-being? Would it serve the young people you steward? If your answer is yes, great!

There's just one catch . . .

Notice and Choose are both cerebral. They live in our minds, and nothing ever changes outwardly because of them. Just noticing that we are not happy doesn't make us happy. Similarly, choosing to be happy doesn't make us happy. Having awareness and setting intentions are great, but often we fall short on the follow-through. They can be like a New Year's resolution: We identify (notice) what we want to do differently or create in a new year, and then we set the intention of (choose) the results we'd like to achieve.

And then . . . 360 days later we notice the same thing. The same resolution is still on the list because the result didn't happen. Have you ever stopped making resolutions because at the end of the year you felt bad that the outcomes you'd resolved for didn't happen? Many of us can identify with this cycle. Another way to think about it is this:

Intention Without Action Is Fantasy!

This brings us to the third step, Act.

Results only happen in action. Our actions determine outcomes. Sometimes the outcomes are what we want them to be, other times they exceed our desires, and sometimes they fall short. Regardless, when we embrace that we are in control of our actions and accept the results that follow, we develop a greater sense of personal agency and self-determination. We model for ourselves and others what accountability and responsibility look like, and we rise to greater versions of ourselves, often in previously unimaginable ways.

When learning Choose and Act, participants sometimes merge or misunderstand the difference between the two. I want to be sure I leave you with clarity that supports your accurate engagement with the NCA framework.

Many training frameworks speak to the power of intention to create results (which I call Choose). They cultivate a belief that intention will get us where we want to be. In the NCA framework a small but mighty shift in perspective changes this belief from the intention being "how" results happen to "what" one wants to happen. What we notice and choose determines the direction of our actions, and those actions determine the results. In the NCA framework, actions need to be three things:

1. Carefully and thoughtfully determined
2. Specific and measurable
3. Practical and attainable

Actions need to be *carefully and thoughtfully determined* to match the results desired. For instance, a teacher looking to improve their self-care by improving quality of sleep might not find much success by simply heading to bed early if they didn't set their life up so their mind could relax.

Actions need to be *specific and measurable*. Clarity is critical so we know exactly what we will be doing and can measure the effectiveness of the action. It is important to use phrases like "I will" and avoid phrases like "I'll try." The action needs to be measurable so it is clear whether it was done or not done as committed. For example, "I will complete all my professional and personal responsibilities by 7:00 p.m. each evening so my mind feels settled as I head to bed by 9:30. If I am unable to complete them by 7:00, I will make a plan to complete them the next day so I am not worrying about it through the night."

Actions need to be *practical and attainable*. If impractical or unattainable, actions will fade into the recesses of our minds and become excuses for why we did not achieve the results we were looking for. This is very personal to each person as we all have different lives and responsibilities. No one knows your day and your story like you do, so only you can determine what is practical and attainable. I invite you to consider that, if it is too easy, it is likely what you are already doing. A growth edge must be a part of the equation. I call this going two steps further than you believe you can or that you want to go. If you typically go to sleep at midnight and get up constantly tired at 6, it might not be practical or attainable to say you will start going to bed by 9:30. However two steps might be turning off all stimulation by 9:30 and heading to bed by 10:30.

Let's look at a few action steps that complete the examples in Notice and Choose.

Educator Actions

- Have a candid conversation with your classes using the SEL Muscles to ask for support solving the struggle.
- Bring contagiously fun and welcoming energy to the classroom—do not let them steal your joy.
- Ask colleagues and administrators for ideas that work for them to engage challenging students.

Parent Actions

- Have a family huddle and share your real feelings using the SEL Muscles and ask for their ideas and support.
- Take small breaks from being responsible for others and take care of yourself. For example, go on a 10-minute walk, relax in a hot shower, or spend 10 minutes on a puzzle you love.
- Learn more about your kids' dreams and share more of your dreams with them.

Using the NCA framework as you seek to shift perspectives, attitudes, actions, and ultimately results will give you an independently designed way forward. The process respects your intelligence and your ability to design your life in ways that make sense to you. Use the framework faithfully at first, exploring what you notice, designing what you choose, and then acting in ways that accomplish your desires. After you begin to experience results that feel great, I expect you will move through the steps quicker and perhaps even a little bit differently. This is not a rigid process; instead, it is a guide for you to master your SEL Muscles and live with more joy and vibrancy, whatever that looks like for you.

Let's dive into the SEL Muscles!

MUSCLE #1

Quit Taking It Personally (QTIP)

INTRODUCTION TO QTIP

The first SEL Muscle, and often the one that lays the groundwork for all the others, is Quit Taking It Personally, also humorously known as QTIP. I think it is safe to say that as parents, guardians, and educators, and in all other roles that are in service to our young, we are deeply invested in their well-being and success. While there are some disputes on the role of the education system in the overall social-emotional-mental well-being of our young people, there typically is agreement that collectively we want our young people to grow into healthy adults. We want them to successfully navigate things like getting and keeping a job; having healthy, happy relationships with partners, family, friends, and coworkers; and being a conscientious citizen, all while having the resilience to overcome disappointments and setbacks that are bound to happen over the course of a lifetime.

Over the last few years we've been blatantly reminded of the need for resilience and the consequences of a lack of it.

We need to be able to navigate the next pandemic, fire, flood, hurricane, or other natural disaster; the next social justice or civil rights movement; constant differences of opinion and lifestyles; and so many other obstacles that range from small to seemingly insurmountable. The consequences that arise from a lack of resilience and tools to move through challenging times are evident in today's statistics: increasing mental illness, increasing hurtful behaviors, increasing attempts and suicide, increasing detachment from social situations, increasing lack of general consideration for other people, and the growing list of untenable conditions.

QTIP is one tool that allows us to personally navigate challenges and in turn teach our young ones to do the same. From the line at the grocery store or behind the too-slow driver, to your relationships with your children, students, colleagues, and families, it is a game-changer.

QTIP FOR EDUCATORS

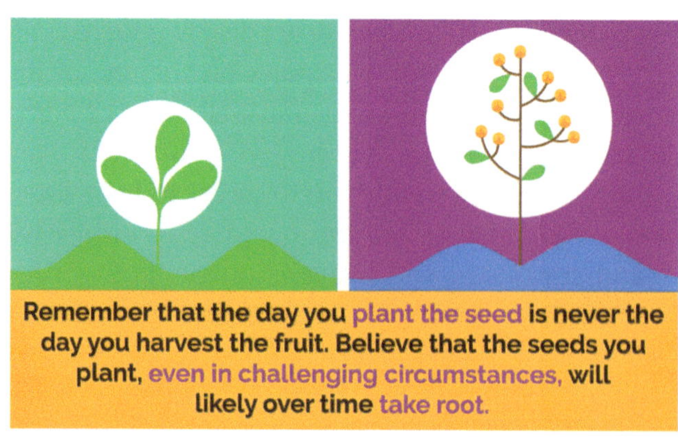

Keeping in mind what we want for our young people and the effort those of us in education make to ensure this outcome, it can feel almost impossible to not take things personally. When our dedicated efforts, both tangible (lesson planning, delivery, grading, meetings, etc.) and in the depth of heart (caring deeply about your students' current and future lives), seem unappreciated, unrecognized, and even challenged, it can feel very personal, even when logically we know that it is not.

Opportunities for us to take specific things personally can exist in any workday, and they can take many forms. It could be a student acting out in class, a parent yelling at you that you're the reason their child isn't performing well, an administrator who makes demands that are outside of your control, or even when you haven't reached a certain student, no matter how hard you've tried. All of these have the potential to disrupt your sense of purpose and success, often resulting in resentment, burnout, and disconnection from the very thing you want: to see your students succeed.

For me, QTIP is the hardest SEL Muscle to keep flexing with strength and conviction. In my first year as a school counselor (in my late 20s), I had an angry mom verbally assault me during a meeting. Every profanity I have ever heard came at me; accusations that I did not care about her daughter reverberated off the walls, her voice just shy of screaming. There was absolutely zero entry point in which I could respond, and to be honest I was shocked. I had worked hours with her daughter trying everything I knew, everything my boss knew, everything her teachers knew, and everything we could all think of that we had never tried before. Her daughter was still truant, failing, and physically aggressive to other students. We weren't giving up; we were trying to bring mom and daughter (she was in the meeting with us) into creative problem-solving.

At that moment, in that meeting, problem-solving was not going to happen. I was shaken up by the barrage, but I was not taking the accusations personally. For me, the behavior from the mother was so egregious that I was able to see that it was not about me. While I had no desire to ever go through that again (the principal and superintendent set new boundaries for her), I also could separate myself from the pain this mom was obviously experiencing and her consequent combative behavior.

However, there were other times when I did take things personally, and the results hampered my joy, my desire to solve problems creatively, and my ability to be the best version of myself both in and out of work. The people who paid for this (outside of myself) were the ones I cared for the most, my family at home. When we are unable to separate ourselves and we take things personally that are not ours to carry, the effects spread in ways that cause additional strain and upset.

Occasionally, there was an adult in my work life who had me personalizing experiences and causing unnecessary upset as a result. There were colleagues who didn't like that I was hired instead of their friend and who worked hard to prevent me from being successful, teachers who gossiped behind my back and insulted me in front of other teachers, and hostile parents who felt it acceptable to use a verbal battering ram to demonstrate their upset. There were times when I was so shocked and "hurt" at their actions—I felt affronted that

1. **they believed I was "against" them or their students rather than "for" them, or**
2. **they would not constructively bring their issues to me directly.**

My responses often included my own little tantrums such as defiant or sulky withdrawal. Of course, the person I was hurting most was me, affecting my moods, my confidence, and my ability to offer my strongest skills, such as creative problem-solving, and bringing my vibrant inclusive personality to all situations. Taking things personally reduced my verve for life and my job, made me less confident, and eroded my happiness, both at home and at work.

After years of practice, I am better at QTIPing, and with each successful flex I feel more ease, joy, and renewed connection to my purpose. I am better able to leave work at work and be a happy grounded person at home. As hard as it may be to remember, the reality is that whatever is coming at us is a statement about the other person's needs and what they are going through, not an indication of anything lacking on our part. We may not be able to diffuse every situation by not taking it personally, but we will be able to move through our days with more ease and peace of mind, which can make a tremendous difference in how our work feels, how our days go, how emotionally stable we are, how much sleep we get, and the list goes on.

At the core of QTIP is giving the benefit of the doubt to others.

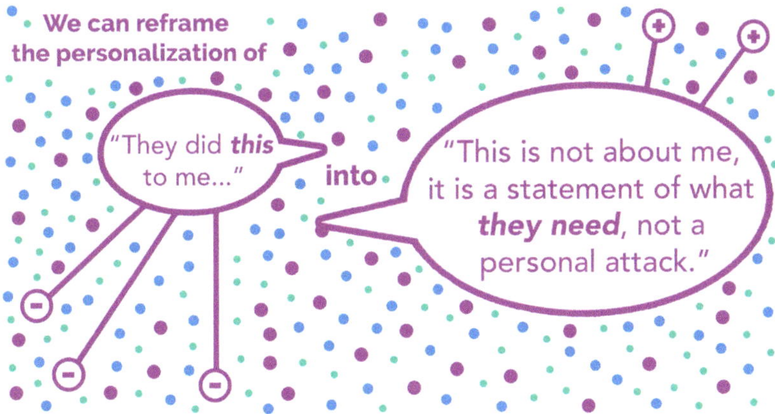

This does not excuse ugly words or behaviors, and it does not dismiss the fact that sometimes boundaries need to be set to mitigate further poor behaviors. In the story of the verbally aggressive mother, boundaries were set, and she no longer had access to anyone without district-level personnel present. We deserved to feel safe, and it was not our problem that she had an issue with it.

The goal is to not tie ourselves up in feeling victimized and defensive. We give grace by offering the assumption that others have needs that we can't always meet. QTIP allows us to move on with our journey without the baggage of the expectations of others, while still being able to care about the humanity of the other person.

Sometimes you may be able to determine motives and what other people need, and sometimes you may have no idea, but it is helpful to remember that even if you don't understand, it's still not about you.

About seven years into my school counselor career I had an amazing opportunity to take a job in a place I wanted to be and work for a woman I wanted to work for. I had three interviews, one with a large team of administrators and teachers at the school site I was applying to. It was nerve-racking, and because I wanted it so much, I added a huge amount of unneeded pressure to the process. In the larger group interview I could feel a bit of unsettling energy, but the overall warmth of the others made the process easier, and I was able to sink into the questions with confidence. I was good at what I did. I was different and creative in my approach with students, and I knew that if they were interested in "outside the box" thinking, I would have the job. I did get the job, and on my first day I was greeted warmly by everyone except my partner in the counseling office. She made it abundantly clear from the start that she was in charge (on paper we were equals), that things needed to be her way (I was hired to be different), and that she was not interested in anything I had to say. Within a few days I was taking it all so personally that I was in tears.

"What did I do?"

"Why doesn't she like me?"

"What can I do to make this better?"

(Backwards somersaults while offering to do all her mundane tasks came to mind.)

This great new job had become a daily barrage of her demands and me trying to dodge them, all while feeling sorry for myself and ill equipped to handle it. It all came down to me feeling pity for myself, which impacted my confidence, which impacted my approach with her, which became an unhealthy cycle. I now look back and shake my head, thinking,

"Oh girl, you were taking her actions personally instead of understanding that she was unhappy that her friend did not get the job. She had a plan, and it didn't happen. This was about her, not about you."

Today I would handle the situation very differently, and I would not take her issues personally. I would use the communication skills I have honed (mostly) by now. In the end it still may not have worked out, but I would have felt better about myself, cried less, not taken the upheaval home with me, been more fun to be around, and not tried so hard to change someone else. I knew in my heart it was not my issue, but I made it about me anyway. About two years in there was a change, and I got a new counseling partner. A few weeks after she started, she sat me down and shared that she was the happiest ever in her new position. She said that she expected to be arriving in a hellish situation, based on what she was told. The final result was good all around for seven years until I left for a new opportunity. I later realized that those two years never had to be so miserable—I did that to myself.

How Often Does the Need to QTIP Show Up in Our Lives?

Whether it is a critical parent or colleague, a seemingly ungrateful young person, or even someone who cuts us off in traffic, doesn't return our call, or seems to not understand our needs, the opportunities to take something personally can rack up. In these situations, and thousands more, our decision to QTIP, or not, equals our ability to tap into our most authentic and joyful selves.

Do our students and children know how to get under our skin? Do they study us for our vulnerabilities and use them against us when they choose to? Do they lash out at us because they have poor coping mechanisms?

The reality is that the answer to all of the questions is yes. Our young people can be unthoughtful and at times even mean; they can trigger us in countless ways, both intentionally and unintentionally. Sometimes they can fail to see our own humanity and the ways that they are baiting us, while at other times they do recognize that we are human and can feel hurt, and they purposely aim for our softest spots.

No matter what they toss at us or how they toss it, if we can remain calm and confident during their storms, many of the upsets that often turn to power struggles can be mitigated or defused.

Because we care so deeply, and we believe in young people's highest potential, hurtful behaviors and words feel *so* personal. But are they? Let's consider this: Whenever we are on the receiving end of upsets that result in hurtful language, attitudes, and behaviors that feel personal, it is a statement about the young (or adult) person's unresolved needs, rather than a statement about any lack on our part. We may not understand the reasons why the student is lashing out, not listening, or failing to follow expectations, but we can know that they, at that moment, do not have the skills, maturity, tools, or understanding to react in a better way. We can offer the benefit of the doubt that they are experiencing gaps in an ability to appropriately handle whatever is happening emotionally inside them. Reasons for this can include what I refer to as a neuro-hijack of the amygdala (the fight, flight, or freeze center of the brain). Sometimes it is learned behavior, and sometimes it's a myriad of reasons all lumped together. Whatever the reason, a person's response is on them.

Understanding this does not mean we are approving the actions that are happening; it simply means we do not have to carry the weighted burden that personalizing creates. This provides the freedom that allows us to approach challenges with greater empathy, patience, and self-care.

SO, NOW WHAT?

If we don't personalize others' behaviors as an attack on us, does that mean we always need to take the proverbial high road? No, we do not. We need to hold our students accountable. Our job goes beyond simply teaching them academic skills. We are guiding them to be caring and conscientious members of society, one where we understand and embrace that our actions can deeply impact others. We do them, and ourselves, a disservice when we let too much slide.

Then there's the "ouch" that we need to be cautious of. This is the slippery slope of disengaging so much from their actions that we excuse ourselves from looking at our own impact and being willing to make shifts that serve us and them. While their actions are a statement of need, our words and actions can be supportive of healthy resolutions for them, or they can be dismissive and cold, like wiping our hands clean and saying, "not my problem." Somewhere, after we calmly realize it is not personal, and before dismissal, is a sweet spot where we can love the person, not take their actions personally, and be a space for that person to safely evolve into a healthier version of themselves.

Therein lies the conundrum: How do we know what to let slide and what to use as teachable opportunities? And how does Muscle #1, QTIP, play into these often split-second decisions?

Educators have always worn many hats that exist outside of the classroom curriculum, such as conflict resolution mediator, recess supervisor, disciplinarian, parent, and so on, and today we add social-emotional and mental health practitioner to the list. We take on so many roles that were not necessarily part of the educator job that we thought we signed up for. Emotional resilience is more necessary than ever in the field of teaching, and your students may push you to limits you had never planned to stretch yourself to. This is why QTIP may be the SEL Muscle that best preserves your mental health and your joy. If you can get good at flexing Muscle #1, you can go home every day with a deeper sense of ease. You can know that

1. you did the best you could at extending understanding and a willingness to reach every student, and
2. you're not letting anything that is "not going right" get under your skin. You're not a miracle worker—you're

a human being in a position with a lot riding on your shoulders, and you deserve to feel as though your efforts are valued and you are doing "enough."

As you know well, teaching is more than just imparting knowledge; it's a profession intertwined with emotions, empathy, and a deep-rooted passion for nurturing growth.

Our students are watching everything we do.

Students notice not just what we say or what we are teaching, but also our attitudes, our ability to be fair and just, who we call on in class—everything! And while they are watching our every move, we cannot begin to keep up with all of them in a similar way. We do what we can to fill in the blanks about what we know about them, and use the information to direct how we interact with them. But we still never know what is truly driving their behaviors. Rationally, we know that the diverse backgrounds and experiences of students contribute to a myriad of emotions, behaviors, and responses within the classroom. What might be considered disrespectful in one culture could be deemed acceptable in another. Ideally, teachers can navigate these cultural nuances without allowing personal sentiments to cloud their judgment. What might be typical behavior for a student can change if something in their life changes (they break up with a boyfriend/girlfriend, their parents are getting divorced, a pet dies, etc.). We do our best to know what is going on with our students—the things that could be affecting their ability to learn and adhere to classroom expectations—but in reality we are just putting some pieces of the puzzle in place while knowing that much of it is a mystery to us. **By practicing not taking it personally, we are protecting our own peace and modeling for our students how to regulate emotions**.

Defensiveness is the great instigator of power struggles. I know that sometimes students can literally work your last nerve,

but if you can often flex the SEL Muscle of not taking it personally, you will find that they cannot affect you as deeply. You can create a necessary buffer for yourself while still validating their experience (this skill is developed in the next SEL Muscles!).

I am certainly not saying it will be easy, but I am definitely saying that it will serve you, and your sanity, well.

Many of us in education feel as though we give and give, and when our work is not honored, not appreciated, and at times even criticized and dismissed, it is hard not to take that personally. But again, you can recognize that a student's inability to see your value because of what they are going through doesn't change how powerfully committed you are. And they may even be seeing your hard work and your efforts but won't let on that they do. If you're teaching middle or high school, you know that adolescence is a turbulent phase marked by hormonal fluctuations, peer pressure, and the quest for identity. These factors, and many more, can cause students to act out, exhibit defiance, and challenge authority figures, not out of malice toward the teacher but as a manifestation of their own inner struggles. Recognizing this helps you avoid internalizing such behaviors as personal attacks.

The ability to detach emotionally from the challenges and setbacks inherent in schools is essential for preserving your mental well-being. Teaching can be emotionally taxing, with educators often bearing the weight of their students' struggles, and their struggles are increasing. By reframing setbacks as opportunities for reflection and growth rather than personal failures, teachers can safeguard their emotional health. This SEL Muscle will most likely require daily flexing, but that is how we create new autopilot habits.

And of course it is not only students who can trigger us. It can be parents, colleagues, administration, policymakers, and the list goes on. Sometimes teachers may face criticism or complaints from parents, and even community members, regarding their teaching methods, grading policies, or interactions with students. While feedback from parents can be invaluable, more and more often it is expressed in aggressive ways, crossing the line of what is appropriate behavior toward another person. While these approaches are hurtful and need to be managed, often with help from leadership, it is essential for educator well-being and effectiveness not to take it personally, as challenging as that is. By not personalizing the other person's poor behavior we have the gift of staying grounded and calm, remaining professional and committed to addressing concerns constructively. If the other party does not meet us there, at least they did not have the power to raise our blood pressure, affect our mood, and derail our promise to cultivate a healthy future for the student in question. Remembering to offer the emotionally reactive parent or carer the benefit of the doubt is important and helps us step back from personalizing the behavior as an affront. Sometimes that can mean repeating statements like these:

Although the statements will be different, we may use them when we encounter conflicts or disagreements with colleagues, whether it's regarding instructional approaches, classroom management strategies, or administrative decisions. In such situations, it's important to recognize that differences of opinion are natural and should be handled with mutual respect and collaboration. In some cases, we may disagree with administrative decisions regarding curriculum changes, scheduling, or disciplinary actions. While it's natural to have personal opinions, it's essential to not take these decisions personally. In all these situations, flexing your QTIP SEL Muscle by focusing on student needs and growth and resisting internalizing external factors as personal affronts is crucial for your well-being and your effectiveness in the classroom.

By reframing setbacks as opportunities for reflection and growth rather than personal failures, teachers can safeguard their emotional health.

QTIP FOR FAMILIES AND CARERS

Can our children push our buttons? Does the sun rise every day? Goodness, our kids can be professional button-pushers (Olympic-worthy ones in fact)! We can't kick them out of class, and there is no principal to send them to. We are the ultimate authority figure, often going it alone, and they can be relentless in their attempts to achieve what they want. So how do we maintain boundaries, rules, and our own sanity?

As a parent myself, I know how challenging it can be to not take things our children (no matter their age) do or say personally. Like every SEL Muscle, some are stronger than others. It has taken me a long time and many setbacks to be good (most of the time) at flexing Muscle #1. Our kids mean the world to us, and we do everything we can, with the tools we have, to navigate their development in ways we hope will set them in the right direction for living a happy, healthy, responsible, resilient, dream-driven life. My grown kids would likely tell you that I took too many things personally and that I was not as effective meeting all their needs as I might have been had I been better at QTIPing. The strategies I developed over decades were born out of a desire to (1) do a better job myself and (2) support other parents and carers in finding successful outcomes. I was fortunate to work with young people and their families and could typically separate myself from taking personally what others did and said better than I could with my own children. When it is so close to home, it feels much more personal, because while we might put heart and soul into others at work, no outcome is truly as important as our own children's well-being. I see you, fellow parents, and I know the value of strengthening this SEL Muscle and the pain of its weakness.

Does this sound familiar to you? You come home after a long day with groceries needing to be unloaded and put away, dinner cooked, homework checked, laundry folded and put away—all the things. You hope beyond hope that when you get home the dishwasher is empty, trash is out, and homework is ready to be checked. You might even feel false hope because you are already resigned to the argument that will happen when those things are not done, and you lose your resolve to stay calm. Or you simply withdraw, do all the things, get a little bit (if lucky) of sleep, and start it all over again in the morning. You think you are good at hiding how deeply personal this is to you, how much resentment is growing, how ineffective you feel as a parent and a person. You want so deeply for your kids to show some care for you as you care so much about them. If they cared, they would certainly want to make your life easier and would do it without being asked, without an argument. Wouldn't they?!

As hard as it can be to remember, your children don't do things because of you; they do things because of them. As personal as it feels—and it can feel *so* personal—it is always about them and what they are struggling to navigate.

Ultimately, this whole thing is nothing but a bunch of "stuff happening," but we rationalize it as a bunch of "stuff happening to us!"

As soon as we identify with it this way, we have given up our power, upending all good communication and learning opportunities, and we act in ways that do not model how we hope our kids will act and speak when they are feeling frustrated, unsupported, and unseen.

We inadvertently put on them, or others, the responsibility for our contentment when we personalize their actions or they watch us do that with others. In exhaustion, overwhelm, high stress, and all the other emotions we feel from time to time (or often), we can easily forget that our kids do not inherently owe us anything. We set the culture of our family. Our moods, words, and actions are what they learn from, and how we navigate expectations and responses is up to us, separate from what they do and say. When we find ourselves saying, "They made me . . . ," we know we are personalizing something and that the results will steal any opportunity for peace of mind and upend our ability to respond to family dynamics with confidence and calm.

Understanding that children go through phases of growth and learning can prevent us from internalizing our child's behavior as a personal attack. The more we know of developmental behavior and general expectations by age range, the more we can separate unrealistic expectations from realistic ones. Of course, this is cerebral information that can get lost in the fray when our child is telling us they hate us, or they are outwitting us with illogical logic. Nevertheless, it is still solid wisdom to lean on when needed, which can be most days.

Another example of a common carer QTIP challenge I heard regularly as a school counselor talking to families revolved around appreciation and expectations. As parents, we offer so much to our children and often have unspoken needs (until we are at our wit's end, and then it doesn't go well) that we assume our kids should know and honor. For instance, we go day after day cooking, cleaning, packing lunches, acting as chauffeur, helping with homework, and supporting hobbies, all while working and trying to maintain some minimal form of personal pursuits. Our kids may not see all of this as something to appreciate; it is just expected to happen. Resentment might build as they ask for more and more without recognizing what they have and how we make it all happen. The "ouch" here is that we create this expectation and then, often in the child's teenage years, come to personalize perceived disregard for our efforts.

At that point the way we communicate pushes them away, and we find ourselves in power struggles. It might sound something like this:

- **"You don't appreciate anything I do for you."**
- **"I do so much for you, and all you do is ask for more and more!"**
- **"After all I do for you, you can't even take out the trash without giving me a hard time?"**

Muscles #2 and #3 will give us additional tools to communicate more effectively in these situations.

At times it can feel extremely personal. Your child can say to you: "You're the worst mother ever! I wish I'd never been born or I'd been born to a different family. I hate you!" This can certainly feel as though it is being directed solely at you, and can feel like it is attacking something with extremely high stakes.

But if you can take a step back and ideally a deep breath (or a few), you can see that your child is lashing out because of something that they need; they're not actually making a harsh commentary on how well you are caring for them. In some cases, what they think they need may be that they don't want to do their homework, they want to stay up late, they don't want to get off their electronics, and so on. You get to play the often unpopular role of "making them do things" that they don't want to do. So although they may lash out at you for it, it is still a statement of them navigating big feelings around not being able to do what they want to, not that you are actually a terrible parent or carer.

QTIP has no guarantees that you can stop these power struggles, but **it can save your sanity**. If you were to take everything personally that your young person directs at you, your nervous system would become compromised in a short period of time. What QTIP ideally does is grant you more serenity and ease. You can become more like a duck: Water literally rolls off their backs, keeping them dry, warm, and afloat. They are able to do this because of a special gland that makes them water resistant. QTIP can act in the same way for you, where you apply it to situations and are able to keep your mental health intact and afloat.

IS IT ALWAYS EASY? NO.

Does it get easier the more that you flex the QTIP SEL Muscle—the more that you apply the awareness that it is not actually about you? Yes. It also lays the groundwork for all the other SEL Muscles that follow, and it can become an SEL Muscle that saves your state of mind, time and time again. While we all can be responsible and continue developing stronger SEL Muscles, it is important to do our best to remind ourselves that our child's behavior is not a direct reflection of how well you are raising and caring for them. Understanding that behavior is separate from a child's inherent value can prevent us from taking negative behaviors personally. Trying to see situations from the child's perspective can help us empathize with their feelings and the motivations behind their behavior. Recognizing that a child's actions are most often driven by emotions, needs, or developmental challenges can assist us from feeling personally attacked.

When our children aren't well regulated, it is our job to remain calm, not join into their agitated state. As the saying goes, be the thermostat, not the thermometer.

BOUNDARIES

Another tool that is game-changing is making sure we set, and hold, boundaries! This one can be hard but is so necessary. Establishing clear boundaries and expectations for behavior (including how appreciations are handled) can help us address challenging behaviors without taking them personally. By focusing on holding the line on boundaries rather than interpreting behavior as a reflection of our skills or an interpretation of what they are, or are not, thinking can help us maintain a sense of objectivity resulting in refined responses that mitigate relationship challenges.

Remember that you are not alone! As families and carers, we can sometimes silo ourselves off, thinking that no one is going through the drama that we are at home. You may even be embarrassed to admit to others how close you can be to your wit's end with a child. Connecting with other families, joining parenting groups, or seeking guidance from counselors or therapists can provide you with validation and support. Sharing experiences with others can help you realize that you are not alone in facing challenges and can offer alternative perspectives. And observing our current statistics, you have plenty of others to find community with.

Just as educators do, families and carers need to examine their own personal triggers. Recognizing our own reactions and emotional responses to our child's behavior can help us to identify any personal triggers or insecurities that may contribute to taking things personally. Developing this self-awareness can give you insight to respond to challenging situations more effectively.

Instead of dwelling on feelings of hurt or frustration, it is helpful to focus on finding constructive solutions to address your reaction and management to your child's behavior. A few ideas on this are here:

1. **Collaborate with your child to problem-solve and develop strategies for managing challenging behavior.**

   This can create a new sense of cooperation and understanding between adults and children. Crazy as it sounds, our children have a hard time seeing us as whole people, not just extensions of themselves. Asking our children their thoughts and their ideas for solutions is powerful and enlightening. They are often harder on themselves than we would ever be once we offer them a space to share openly.

2. **Ask others what they think, and ask them to be honest.**

   While this initially may feel risky and vulnerable, the insights of others we trust (they will love us and our kids even when things go wrong) or respect (they have street and/or professional credibility that gives them knowledge and separation to see things more clearly than we can when we are swimming in the muddy waters of emotional upset and paralyzed into doing nothing in fear of doing it wrong) are invaluable. Asking others develops trust and collaboration, easing the journey and making it feel much less lonely.

TAKE CARE OF YOURSELF

I know it can be so hard, as sometimes we barely feel like we can go to the bathroom by ourselves or we tiptoe to prevent any kind of upset. It is essential to find time for some kind of self-care. If you know what you love most, what soothes you best, be sure to fit some of it in. If you don't know, try some things out, and find some tools that bring respite and ease. Too often we think that we have no time to spare, but it is as important for us to take care of ourselves as it is for our children to see us doing so. I know it is trite, but there is solid logic behind the notion of putting your own oxygen mask on before you can help others. Parenting has transformed into an ever-vigilant job, and in order to keep up with all that is happening in the world and in our homes without breaking down, we must find ways to manage stress and maintain our emotional resilience. Taking care of our own well-being can prevent us from becoming overly reactive or taking our child's behavior personally. It also models for them to do the same.

QTIP CAUTIOUS CONSIDERATIONS

There are some cautionary tales of QTIP that can be challenging to recognize as we work diligently to improve our ability to stay emotionally unattached to what someone else says, does, or believes.

Caution #1: Actually Doing It

While we may be able to "see" that not taking something personally would benefit us and offer language (in our own mind and out loud), the slippery slope is managing our emotional response. Knowing what would be best in the situation for our own sanity and peace of mind does not always translate to doing what will bring ease and comfort as the situation ends. It is important to translate understanding into action. This is where flexing must be practiced because, like every muscle in our body, simply thinking we want to be stronger does not alleviate atrophy.

Educator

A student refuses to do any homework, rarely passes tests, and is in danger of failing your class. You have offered to meet them at lunch or after school, to help them get on track. You have called home to discuss your concerns for this student, and you have spoken to administration and counseling about your concerns. You are at your wit's end. However, you can flex your QTIP SEL Muscle and see that this is not about you. There must be more to this student's story than you know. You have the tools, awareness, and language to apply QTIP. You've got this!

And then, you bark at the student, or you give the student the cold shoulder, finding yourself feeling frustrated more than caring. You might not even notice that the student is costing you a subtle (or not so subtle) price for not engaging more with their own outcomes, after all you have done for them. You seem to care for them more than they care about themselves, and this can be discouraging and exhausting. Your own emotional health is taxed, and while you might justify your mood, it is simply impossible to be proud of it.

Now, you might become frustrated at the QTIP SEL Muscle because it is not working—you are still not at peace even though you want to be. In that awareness you have the opportunity to give yourself grace, acknowledge that this is a long game of SEL Muscle strengthening, and recognize that the workout is worth it, no matter how long it takes to build the SEL Muscle. Why? Because you and your peace of mind are *worth* it. Because when you go home feeling solid rather than taken out, your evening (and those you share it with) will get the best of who you are rather than the frustrated and depleted version of yourself.

Perhaps one of the hardest things to do in approaching QTIP is to allow yourself room to be wrong, or room for growth. When we are 100% committed to being right, looking good, or the consistent notion that "I got this," there is no room for not taking it personally. QTIP inherently requires us to see outside of ourselves and offer benefit of the doubt to the other person.

IDEAS

- When a student demonstrates not caring, a QTIP response might sound like "I hear you, and no problem—I can care enough for us both until you are able to meet me."
- When a colleague tells you what "should" work with a student, or how they "don't have that problem" (aka, they "do it better than you"), a QTIP response might sound like "That is awesome—maybe I could observe you sometime?" or "I wonder if you could share a couple of your success stories with me."

These responses are apt to diffuse any developing struggles because you let go of the full control of the situation while still maintaining your integrity, strength, and well-being.

Parent/Carer

You are knee deep and exhausted as you move through responsibilities at home, at work, for children, for your significant other, for extended family, for your community, for your friends, and so on. You feel like you have it together, until you don't. You need support, and you ask your child to do an age-appropriate thing: pick up a few toys, empty a dishwasher, put away clean clothes, start a meal, carry in items you shopped for . . . The list is long because the tasks are many. You believe that your request is simple, until you are ignored or argued with or the negotiations begin.

Knowing they are young, you feel like you can give them the benefit of the doubt and flex your QTIP SEL Muscle. You think you aren't taking their pushback personally, as you stay cool and try again, and again, and again. At some point the "and again" drives you over the edge, and the result is not something you feel good about. For example, you do the task yourself, you engage in a power struggle, or you get them to do it but everyone is mad, and the house is in chaos. *And*, you feel terrible inside, defeated, unsupported, devalued, ineffective, and maybe even unloved.

All this is going on inside you while you're also experiencing the guilt of "losing it" or frustration over "giving in." In those moments it is easy to forget your QTIP SEL Muscle (this isn't about me; it is about them). Any unfavorable reaction by us toward them demonstrates our attachment to their actions over our own calm and ease. We often attach the following ideas to our kids, and when they don't meet the expectation, we take it personally even though we have set them up for the exact response we are upset by. This can be hard to recognize and an "ouch" to wrap our head around.

IDEAS

- **"I do so much for you, so the least you can do is . . ."** Even if these specific words are not spoken, this mindset takes their action/inaction very personally and requires a young person to "pay you back" for being their parent/carer. This

continued

continued from previous

will not create a long-term healthy outcome for either party. A statement that may address the situation without personalizing it may be "I hear that you aren't interested in taking out the trash, and I never am either. That said, I need help. Without help I am grouchy and exhausted. This is bad for us all." Sharing with your child what you need (more on this in other SEL Muscles) and making sure the task is identified as *not* an option are clear ways to communicate what you need from them. Even if they do not respond in a way you want, you can feel good about your approach.

- **"Would you take out the garbage?"** This question leaves room for a person to simply refuse. We think we have been polite and they "should" want to do what we ask because we said please. When they don't do what we "asked," we take it personally, even going so far at times to associate their noncompliance with personalizations such as "They don't love me," "They don't care about me," or "Can't they just see I need help?"

All of this creates reactions that are often void of positive outcomes because we have identified their actions as the reason for our upset. When we recognize this, we can become better at flexing our QTIP SEL Muscles and replace challenging interactions with calm ones. This does not mean you get your way every time, but it does mean you feel good about yourself and your effort to create environments that you feel positive in.

Caution #2: What We Need to Hear

This one can be a bit of an "ouch" because not many of us love it when we need to hear and embrace things that identify our areas of growth. Take a deep breath and allow yourself to really let this sink in.

There are times when what others are telling us—maybe our student, our boss, our partner, our best friend, our child, or a parent—will actually help us improve. We can become more creative educators, better friends, more competent workers, more collaborative team players, more compassionate listeners, calmer parents . . . You get the idea. None of us live in a vacuum, and all of us have room to develop. When we are receiving feedback, it is important to be able to distinguish between what is ours to receive and what is about others.

For instance, your colleague is feeling frustrated because you were late to a meeting for the third time. The colleague is speaking with irritation when addressing you. You determine that the irritation is on the other person; however, you are the one experiencing upset, and therefore the solution can be found in your actions. It would be supportive of the relationship to acknowledge that you were late and that you realize this created an inconvenience for the colleague. Often, however, an irritated person is met with an irritated reaction, and this simply escalates the situation, and resolution is missed all together.

Another example might be with a teenager at home or in class. An assignment is given that the teenager doesn't understand the reasoning behind. They get edgy (that may be a kind word for how they act) and escalate to a state of refusal. As an educator or a parent, it might be helpful for us to offer reasoning to some requests. However, sometimes we ourselves escalate to an immediate power struggle. As adults, we feel that we should be respectfully listened to. The longer we personalize rather than get on board with today's youth and how to reach them, the more frustrated and ineffective we will be. Frustrated and ineffective is a perfect combination to create stress and unhappiness. Leaning into learning about others and being curious about what they might be contributing to us will lead to less personalization and deeper, more meaningful relationships—including the one we have with ourselves.

QTIP Review

THE BASICS

- QTIP stands for "Quit Taking It Personally."
- QTIP is a mental strategy to avoid personalizing negative interactions.
- Others' actions reflect their needs and lived experiences, not your worth.

WHY BOTHER?

- QTIP helps maintain emotional stability and mental health.
- QTIP allows for more empathetic and effective responses.
- QTIP prevents burnout and resentment in both familial and educational settings.

SECRET SAUCE

- Reframe negative interactions from "They did this to me" to "This is about their needs."
- Give the benefit of the doubt to others: "There is something I do not know."
- Separate "personal feelings" from "what is happening."

AWESOME OUTCOMES

- Develop emotional resilience in challenging situations and interactions.
- Preserve mental health and reinvigorate joy in our roles with young people.
- Create more positive and productive atmospheres at home, in classrooms, and in communities.

TIPS FOR SUCCESS

- **Reframe negative interactions:** Shift your perspective by recognizing that others' behaviors reflect their own needs, challenges, or emotions rather than being a direct attack on you. This mindset helps preserve emotional stability and allows for more empathetic and confident responses.
- **Set boundaries while staying objective:** Establish clear boundaries to address inappropriate behaviors without personalizing them. Focus on maintaining objectivity and holding others accountable in a constructive way, which can reduce stress and improve relationships.

- **Practice self-care and emotional resilience:** Regularly engage in self-care to maintain your emotional well-being, enabling you to respond calmly and confidently in challenging situations. This not only protects your mental health but also models emotional regulation for others, such as children or students.

QTIP Pause and Reflect

NOTICE.

- In what areas of life do you take things personally? Who or what feels the most personal?
- When you feel personally affronted, what feelings do you experience? What behaviors, words, or attitudes follow these feelings?
- Who is most affected by these behaviors? What does it cost you and those you care about? What does it cost you as you move through your day, regardless of who you are around?

CHOOSE.

- Considering what you notice, what outcomes would you prefer instead?
- What can you see about yourself and your relationships if you could step back from personalizing and step into offering grace to yourself and others?
- How would you be feeling, and what behaviors, words, and actions would you experience in yourself? Who would benefit from this new approach?

ACT.

- What mindset, words, or actions will you apply to reduce personalizing what others present? Be specific and realistic.
- Maybe consider these starters:
    - As I notice myself feeling triggered, I will immediately . . .
    - When I step back from my reaction to others, I am able to . . .
    - After I get triggered and I notice this happened, I will . . .

Consider possible obstacles to these actions and prethink a plan to overcome them.

Remember to give yourself room to get it right and miss it fully—it's the practice that moves us forward.

SILENT STRUGGLES
DESERVE LOUD
SUPPORT.
ALL IT TAKES.

MUSCLE #2

The Power of "I"

INTRODUCTION TO THE POWER OF "I"

The Power of "I," the second SEL Muscle, is a powerful tool to use in everyday conversations with all people. It is particularly useful when a conversation needs to take place that involves either real or perceived conflict. The Power of "I" changes the dynamic of "power over" and "accusation" to "in it together" and "problem-solving." The result is a sense of relief and personal care while offering those same experiences to the other people we are in communication with. Whether speaking to other adults or young people, the opportunity is the same: a chance to be responsible for ourselves and our impact on others while proactively communicating needs and working to achieve a mutually beneficial outcome. Even if the outcome is not what is most desired, the outcome holds each person with respect and care.

I have been told by teachers and parents that the term *"I" statement* sounds like a psychologically touchy-feely approach that gives over their power and undermines their authority. The good news is that "I" statements actually support credibility, build trust, and help maintain authority rather than undermine it. The invitation is for you, the reader, to approach this chapter with an open and curious mind. As you read, consider yourself in the examples. Do you relate to any of the statements?

THE POWER OF "I" FOR EDUCATORS

Initially, just reading or hearing the term *"I" statements* prevents some of us educators from being willing to dive into the process, explore the results, and measure, for ourselves, the actual outcomes versus our preempted perceived ones.

"I" statements can instantly defuse the power struggle that is about to happen, and as we all know, that can come into play quite often in educational settings, with both students and colleagues. Typically, challenges pop up between people because of a pretty standard X-then-Y formula. You can fill in the blanks with whatever conflict is at hand.

"Because you did X, my life is Y!"

"Because X happened, I did/said Y."

"If it weren't for X, then I would have been able to Y."

The X-then-Y factor can be never-ending and is generally a catalyst that creates power struggles, conflict, and unhappy relationships. And what is the general response to statements, like those given earlier, that place blame on someone else? Defense mechanisms kick in! When they do, they make it that much more difficult for anyone to get what they want. In general, the person on the receiving end of "You did X!" becomes defensive, and in return the accusatory person becomes equally defensive. Then it is just a standoff, with both people digging in their heels more and more. Productive communication and calm resolution is more out of reach than before the exchange started.

When we express what we need, what we want, and what we are experiencing through an "I" statement, we are far more able to make progress in the situation at hand. We are able to create openings for others to hear us, and consequently feel recognized, seen, and heard—things that everyone wants to feel. We offer opportunities for others to relate to us, rather than for them to be put on the defensive and most likely not hear or understand what we are actually trying to say. We operate in a problem-solving mentality, not trying to determine who is at fault, but aiming to create some resolution and understanding. "I" statements allow us to own what we are experiencing, without blaming someone else for it and lighting the fuse of a combative power struggle. In power struggles everyone loses, but with an "I" statement there is potential for all parties to feel heard and have their experience validated.

For example, it may be the 10th time that a student has disrupted your class on a particular day. You have tried the usual methods—patiently asking them to stop, pausing the lesson, waiting silently while blatantly giving them "that look," and all the other tools in your arsenal. Nothing is working, and you find yourself saying things like this:

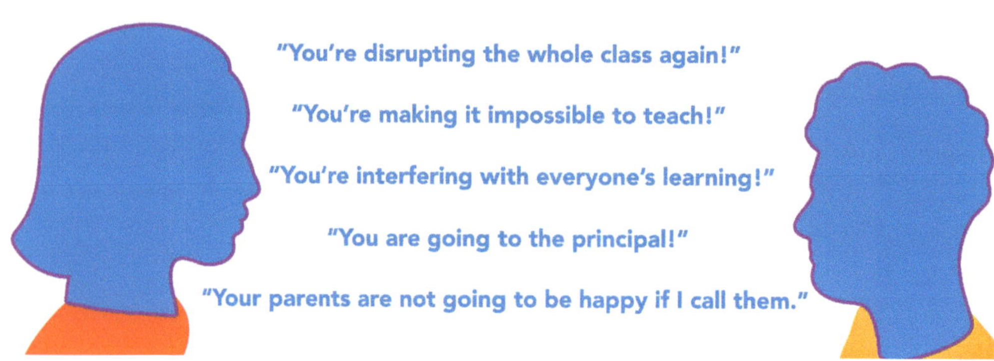

Trying to shut down behavior by threatening or negotiating erodes trust and compromises relationships. Both undermine opportunities for collaborative problem solving and often escalate power struggles or drive isolating behaviors.

In this moment, you remember that you now have a new tool, a new SEL Muscle to flex. You take a deep and necessary breath and try an "I" statement.

"What I'm experiencing right now is frustration because I can't find a way to meet your needs and at the same time teach the whole class. I am feeling unsuccessful because I care about both what's going on with you and teaching to everyone. Would you be willing to let me finish the lesson and then come check in with you as soon as I can, like 5 minutes? I feel confident we can find a way to get you what you need. Can I count on your patience and you count on me checking in with you?"

Of course, we know that nothing is fail-safe, but the potential for this to shift the situation is far higher than if you threw out the typical responses, which often come off as accusatory jabs.

You are allowing the students (as they are all watching this play out) to see you as a multidimensional person with needs too. Often students fail to see their teachers as real people, with emotions just as powerful as their own. Typically, this is how many teachers establish the dynamic, one of distance and professionalism, with their students. While this certainly has its place in teacher–student relationships, there is also tremendous value in letting down the wall in appropriate instances and showing your students your humanity, your wishes, and your desires too.

By using "I" statements, you release others from any blame and put the focus on problem-solving together, ideally with everyone getting at least some of what they want.

Be sure to follow through! If you tell a student what they can count on from you, you must make good on it. Little loses credibility faster than a teacher telling a student what they will do and then failing to keep their word. You can also practice flexing Muscle #2 in lower-stakes situations so that everyone becomes familiar with the dynamic. For example, if the class is particularly squirrelly one day, you can stop the lesson and address it. "I am experiencing that a lot of you are feeling extra squirmy today. I am feeling that way too, but we have some things we need to get through. Can I ask that we all focus and I will finish the lesson 5 minutes early so we can have a 'rock paper scissors' contest to see who will lead us to lunch?" Obviously, this would be for younger students, but you could modify the incentive for any age. The more that your students become accustomed to experiencing you as trying to work with them, rather than judging them or jumping to threatening talk and punitive measures, the further it will go at creating relationships where they will want to cooperate more often.

We have triggers as much as our students do—often even more so because we've lived long enough to pick up many. Our triggers exist for a multitude of reasons, and this is why Muscle #2 needs flexing. Our triggers are on autopilot, so this SEL Muscle needs to disrupt and combat long-held patterns. A way to keep practicing and reinforcing the new approach with students and colleagues is to actually speak, in real time, what you are experiencing even when you miss using an "I" statement and fall back into a "you" statement.

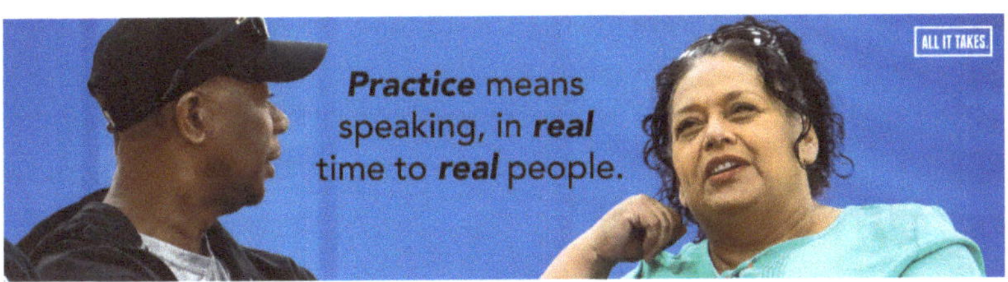

A "you" statement can sound like this:

"You didn't do your homework again! Oh, wait, I apologize—let me try that again. I see that you don't have your homework to turn in. I am wondering if you will meet me at break so we can work together to find a way for you to have success with homework. I imagine if I am feeling challenged by this, it must be worse for you. I want to understand and support. Can I count on you to join me at break so we can work this out together?"

Another way I like to look at requests to try again is to ask for a "do-over." For example:

Instead of "I apologize—let me try that again," you could say, "That didn't come out right—can I have a do-over?"

Students love it when an adult owns their missteps. We ask young people to do this all the time, and it is trust-building to do the same ourselves. If we ask for a do-over by first acknowledging that something wasn't right, we are owning our behavior, and for most people (young people included) this is what is most important.

Do-overs are a great tool to teach and allow students to use. Do-overs give the space for the initial "autopilot" response to happen and then provide a self-reflective opportunity to try again. Do-overs allow for an intentional replacement behavior without a power struggle, shame, or blame. Also, once taught, do-overs can be indicated with a silent signal rather than spoken word. This again avoids the opportunity for a power struggle, as illustrated by the following example from my days as an elementary school counselor.

When the lunch bell rang, students would come racing down the halls, pushing past one another, screaming with wild abandon, toward the cafeteria. This happened every day without fail even though all students knew the rules:

No running in the hallways

No cutting or pushing in line

No screaming inside

I heard myself, and every other adult in the area, raising our voices above the fray:

"Stop running!"

"You are not supposed to run in the halls!"

"Stop pushing and shoving—you are breaking the hands-off rule."

"WALK!"

I get tired of hearing myself say redundant things that are already known yet I know will be ignored. Ineffectiveness turns to frustration, which turns to barely contained yelling, which ultimately never stopped students from running in the halls, day after day. Then I thought of do-overs, and everything changed when I was around.

I started pulling aside the high-flyer runners first. I explained to them that from now on when I saw them running I would signal to them with my finger pointing up and turning in a circle, in a do-over rotation. When they saw this, they had to walk all the way back to where they started and then walk back toward the cafeteria. The first time I did this, I actually walked them back to their starting point. Then they ended up at the very back of the lunch line.

This worked like magic. If they saw me, they were walking because they knew that a do-over put them at the back of the line. No one raised their voice, and students were safer and considered what they wanted more: to run or to be at the back of the line. Another benefit of this was that they were purposeful in their actions rather than impulsive, and this helped develop their self-regulation skills. Finally, because I did this with the most influential students first, it had a calming trickle-down effect, reducing hallway traffic and chaotic lunch lines.

Overall, the power of using "I" statements lies in our ability to promote self-expression, understanding, and respectful dialogue in interpersonal interactions. They serve as a valuable tool for effective communication, de-escalation, accountability, empathy-building, problem-solving, and conflict resolution both for you and for your students. Imagine you're in your classroom filled with eager students, each with their own unique perspectives and experiences. As an educator, you understand the importance of fostering open communication and creating a supportive learning environment. You decide to incorporate the use of "I" statements as a teaching tool to help your students express themselves effectively.

You begin by explaining the concept of "I" statements to your students, highlighting how you are going to start using "I" statements and how they can use these statements to express their thoughts, feelings, and needs in a respectful and assertive manner. You share examples of "I" statements in action, emphasizing how the students can use them to promote empathy, understanding, and positive dialogue with their peers and the adults in their lives. You explain it in terms that will be relatable and ideally show them how effective "I" statements can be in their own lives. The following are a few examples you can share with them that demonstrate a typical approach and then an "I" statement approach. Ask them, after every share, which one of these statements is most likely to end up in a productive conversation.

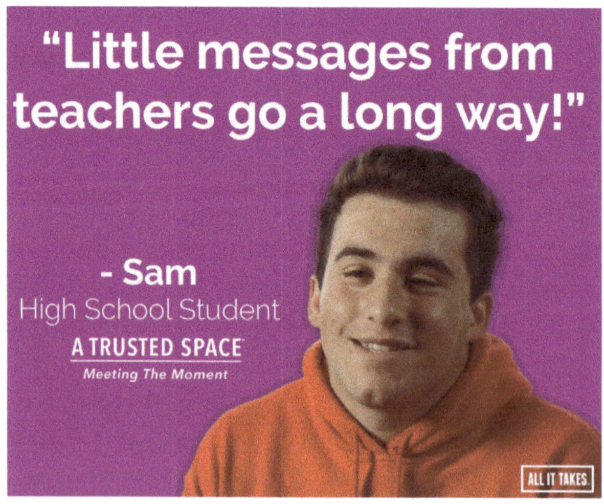

Scenario: A younger student is trying to enjoy recess and is facing obstacles on the swings.

"It's *my* turn on the swings, so you have to get off . . . I'm telling!"

"I feel sad that I have not had a turn on the swings. I want to have fun too, so can you give me a turn?"

Scenario: A teenager feels insecure about how to do an assignment so they don't turn it in.

"You didn't explain it. You didn't even teach it!" Or, to a parent: "My teacher hates me. They wouldn't even help me, and they want me to fail."

"I really don't understand this assignment, but I want to do well. Can you help me?"

Scenario: A parent changes the family schedule and disrupts a teenager's plans with friends.

"You always ruin my plans. You don't care about me!"

"I had plans with my friends, and this last-minute change is really hard for me to accept. Is there anything we can do so I can still see my friends?"

The most important tool you have in your kit is your own practice in front of and with your students. Ask them to start noticing when you use an "I" statement and to let you know when they notice. When this happens, celebrate them, or give whatever positive recognition you use in your education community or classroom. Remember, we build our SEL Muscles by flexing them first!

As the days go by, hopefully you will observe your students putting this concept into practice. During class discussions, instead of pointing fingers or placing blame, they use "I" statements to share their perspectives. If they are having trouble catching on, continue to guide them to shift from "you" to "I." If it seems appropriate, you can explain how just like the muscles in our bodies, it takes time to develop our SEL Muscles and get used to communicating in that way.

Here are few ways to remind students to use "I" statements:

When a student starts a sentence with "you," your response can be "Who, *me*?" or, simply, "Who?" This can be done humorously. Use a fun voice, asking them, "Who are you talking about, yourself or me?" Once they start to catch on, there will be shifts in their language.

Another way to support them in using an "I" statement is simply saying something like this:

"That is a 'you' statement. Can you try again using an 'I' statement?"

Miraculously, this has a huge added benefit for students who are typically complainers. What happens is they love to complain and get people to join them in their upset. When they approach you to complain about someone else and you ask them to rephrase it using an "I" statement, they often don't want to bother and will simply walk off and handle their own stuff. On the playground this is especially effective when used by campus supervisors.

You'll notice a shift in the classroom dynamic. Students feel more empowered to express themselves authentically, believing that their feelings are being acknowledged and respected. This creates a sense of trust and camaraderie among classmates, which in turn fosters a supportive learning community. Students may not be able to articulate the change, but they will feel it. As we know, our students' feelings drive the majority of their actions, attitudes, and words, especially since their amygdalae are still mostly running the proverbial show.

For added support of what happens in a young person's brain and how the amydala can hijack the best of intentions, you can watch

A Trusted Space: Decoding Behavior for adults or ***A Trusted Space: Navigating Storms*** for youth.

These can be found at **atrustedspace.org** and are free to access.

When conflicts arise, you can encourage them, like you do yourself, to use "I" statements to communicate their feelings and find common ground. This approach helps to de-escalate tensions and promotes constructive problem-solving skills.

As the school year progresses, you will see the impact of incorporating "I" statements into your teaching practice. For yourself you will begin to see your students respect and trust you at a deeper level. You will find yourself feeling more balanced and happy because there will be fewer power struggles and more successes, even if small at first. Your students will not only become more confident communicators but also develop a deeper understanding of themselves and others. Ideally, they carry these valuable communication skills beyond the classroom, applying them in their personal relationships and school experiences.

I have a colleague who grew up with a mother who taught her about "I" statements back in the '70s, long before they were part of popular theory. She readily admits to disliking the practice when she was young (today she is grateful), saying that if she had a dollar for every time she groaned, "I know, I know, use an 'I' statement," while rolling her eyes as a teenager, she would have amassed a small fortune.

So are our students always going to be receptive to this shift in communication? Of course not! Are our students always going to be receptive to anything they don't intrinsically want to do (eat pizza, be on their devices, etc.)? Again, of course not, but we keep at it. Don't take it personally if it takes some time to catch on, and do be mindful of pressing the issue so hard that they develop resistance to it, as my colleague did. However, even she is aware that it took root in her rebellious teenage mind. Although she wouldn't have admitted it to her mother, she knew that, in the long run, the practice has served her well.

Through your role as an educator, you can empower your students with a powerful tool for effective communication and conflict resolution. You know that your students learn just as much through interactions and trial and error at being a human as they do with academics. "I" statements have a remarkable ability to defuse conflicts by shifting the focus from blame and accusation to personal feelings and experiences. In the world of children and teenagers and their very real and often heightened emotions, this can save friendships and reputations and reduce chances for embarrassment and power struggles. If packaged correctly, your students can see how this SEL Muscle works in their favor. By embracing "I" statements, they can learn to express themselves assertively, empathize with others, and build stronger connections both inside and outside the classroom.

Remember, this is especially true if the young people see you successfully using the tool!

THE POWER OF "I" FOR FAMILIES AND CARERS

"I" statements are game-changers within families. They can shift dynamics from constant power struggles where essentially no one feels like they're getting their needs met to a home where communication goes well more often and family members are more interested in communicating with one another. We may feel impatient and wish all of the SEL Muscles could be developed immediately, but it is important to keep in mind that we're working toward progress, not perfection! It took us decades to get to this point—decades of us being children learning from our parents, and now being parents trying to do it better while unraveling old autopilot ways and reestablishing new norms of behavior and attitudes.

Using the Power of "I," or "I" statements, is critical for the development of a healthy and productive communication style within a family. *Nowhere do we feel more compelled to get it right and yet so quickly revert to old ways and patterns.* For most of us parents, using "you" statements is both learned behavior and habit. "You" statements are used frequently when we have just taken something personally and are in a reactive state of perceived self-preservation. We can have the best-laid plans for our family to live and communicate harmoniously, and then it can all go to pieces over the wrong kind of cereal or a party that you won't allow your child to attend. And everything in between!

Communication within families is often fraught with the potential for blow-ups and power struggles, as the age-old line from kids is, **"You just don't understand me!"** It is part of the natural developmental stages for young people to rebel against their families and carers, and that rebellion can take many forms. At times it can feel extremely personal when your child says things like this:

continued

continued from previous

"You're the worst mother ever! I wish I'd never been born or I'd been born to a different family. I hate you!"

"All my friends have cool parents, but you are just trying to ruin my life!"

"You don't care about me!"

Ouch—there is no one we care more about than our children, and frankly, many times they know this when they say such things. This can certainly feel as though it is being directed solely at you, and can feel like it is attacking something with extremely high stakes.

Keeping in mind that all the SEL Muscles build on themselves, how does one use an "I" statement in combination with QTIP to feel secure in addressing children or teens?

A few simple approaches can keep us true to ourselves while honoring them, resulting in reduced power struggles, less chaos, fewer upsets, more joy, and more productive conversations:

1. Remember that what is happening is not personal. What they are upset about is not about you; it is about them (repeat and repeat again).
2. Work to understand what is missing for them—what they need—and ask them or reflect that back to them starting with an "I" statement.
3. Keep in mind that young people often do not discern the difference between want and need, and you will have to teach them over time how to tell the difference.
4. Help your kids learn to distinguish between having an opinion and getting their way.
5. Wrap all these elements in your cultivation of an "I" statement.

"Blood pressures differ among 40-year-olds depending on what happened to them in 5th grade."

- Valerie Shapiro, PhD

AN EXAMPLE OF THIS FROM WHEN I WAS RAISING MY KIDS

My daughter came home from sixth grade one day with a flyer and an enthusiastic bounce in her step. The local bowling alley was having an overnight "lock-in." The invited ages were 12–17, and the plan was to have an overnight bowling party where no one could leave after arrival. Nor could anyone enter past a certain time. Sponsored by the bowling alley and our community's parks and recreation department, the event assured parents that there would be plenty of supervision and fun for all. My daughter was all over it, super excited and telling me how many of her friends were planning to go.

My brain and mom's sense was "What are you talking about?" An overnight in a bowling alley with 17-year-olds, no sleep, no supervisors I knew, and 100 other thoughts that did not align with her excitement filled my head.

My daughter was incredibly compelling. Often I would question my own sanity as I listened to her argument and was drawn into her reasoning. This did not always support me, or her, or our relationship, and I learned a lot about myself and how I gave over my power in many situations (not just with her). Listening to her in this instance, I wasn't feeling safe about the whole situation. Additionally, I thought, "If we allow her to participate in a 'lock-in' overnight at 12 years old, what in the world will we have to say yes to when she is 16?"

When I shared with her my concerns, of course she had a counter-concern regarding each of mine. I was able to use "I" statements that allowed me to share my concerns without criticizing the event or her desire to attend it with

continued

continued from previous

her friends. I was also able to separate from personalizing her disappointment. Also I was clear that what she needed was to be a part of her social group and feel included. I understood that what she wanted at the moment was about her social group and that saying no compromised her perception, or even reality, of acceptance from them.

I was able to feel good about both saying no and talking about my reason. Her upset was not my responsibility to own, and yet I could still offer, and legitimately feel, compassion for the disappointing news she received when I said no.

You might notice based on my story that a lot of "I" statement work is internal. Using "I" when reflecting on how to address an issue rather than the unspoken finger-wagging "you" keeps us responsible for our next steps and words. It keeps us calmer and in problem-solving mode rather than attack mode. Our selves and our young people benefit when we use the Power of "I"!

There is quite a bit of research and thought on the use of "I" statements. In the 1960s, Thomas Gordon highlighted the concept of an "I" statement as a tool to replace "you" statements, which usually put the blame on and attribute the issue to the listener. "I" statements, or what I like to call the Power of "I," have evidentiary support for their success in many personal and business settings (see Gordon, n.d.).

A psychological principle termed the norm of reciprocity describes a basic human tendency to match the behavior and communication style of one's partner during social interaction (Rogers et al., 2018). During conflict, a hostile approach typically produces hostility in return from the other person, potentially creating a negative downward spiral. In brain science, this can also be associated with mirror neuron responses where the affect of one person is taken on by another person (see www.allittakes.org/atrustedspace/educatorinsights). This mood-matching, if you will, is true in both supportive and unsupportive environments, which is why learning to communicate with de-escalating language, harnessing the Power of "I," is helpful in psychological and neurological outcomes. "I" statements have the power to avoid escalating situations and also to pull a charged situation back to a place of productive conversation that supports positive outcomes. Communicated in terms of personal experiences, perspectives, and emotional states, "I" statements avoid accusatory approaches that rarely end well.

When you are in conflict, you may have difficulty clearly articulating your situation without escalating the conflict. Using an "I" statement can help you state your concerns, feelings, and needs in a manner that is easier for the listener to hear and understand.

An "I" statement focuses on your own feelings and experiences. It does not focus on your perspective of what the other person has done or failed to do. It is the difference, for example, between saying "You never take advantage of my offers for extra help, and that is why you are failing," and "I am concerned about you passing my class, and I would like to talk about what it will take from both of us for you to find success."

If you can express your experience in a way that does not attack, criticize, or blame others, you are less likely to provoke defensiveness and hostility, which tends to escalate conflicts, or have the other person shut down or tune you out, which tends to stifle communication.

WHAT AN "I" STATEMENT DOES

An "I" statement can help reduce blaming, accusations, and defensiveness.

An "I" statement can help you communicate your concerns, feelings, and needs without blaming others or sounding threatening. It helps you get your point across without causing the listener to shut down.

An "I" statement says, "This is how it looks from my side of things." In contrast, consider the following "you" statements:

"You are lazy. You expect me to give you a passing grade when you make no effort."

continued

continued from previous

"You are disruptive. You are never paying attention and make it hard for others to do so."

"You don't ask questions, and then perform poorly. How can I help you if I don't know what's wrong?"

Sound familiar?

Arguments about homework, behavior, and attitude are nothing new. In fact, for many educators and their students, they may create frequent points of contention. That's exactly why "I" statements are so important. Choosing the right words during an argument can be the difference between resolving your issues and making them worse. **When you change your words, you change your life**, and nowhere is this truer than in relationships, of all kinds.

Even when you have the best of intentions, what you say can escalate an exchange and damage a relationship, consequently reducing or eliminating trust. And one of the most common mistakes often made is the use of "you" statements instead of using sentences that are framed as "I" or "I feel" statements.

What Is a "You" Statement?

"You" statements, such as those listed earlier, are phrases that begin with the pronoun *you* and imply that the listener is responsible for something. They show no ownership of emotions, but rather blame the receiver. This type of statement is more likely to make your partner feel defensive and resentful, and they will be less likely to want to make peace.

What Is an "I" Statement?

An "I" statement, on the other hand, forces us to take responsibility for what we are thinking and feeling and prevents us from blaming our partners. When using "I" statements, we can still be assertive, but find a less hostile, more compassionate way to communicate.

Tone of voice—vocal inflection, volume, and pitch—is an important piece of the communication puzzle that we often forget about. "I" statements help prevent miscommunication that can happen when one partner takes an accusatory tone of voice.

The Psychology Behind "You" Statements and "I" Statements

Studies have shown that "I" statements reduce hostility and defensiveness and that "you" statements can provoke anger. Today it's a commonly accepted fact that the use of "I" statements in relationships and even at work results in better communication. But why?

"You" statements" make your partner feel that you are punishing them. When people feel attacked, they naturally become defensive. It seems to be hardwired into our DNA. By pointing out what they've done wrong or how they've made you feel upset, sad, or angry, you're either trying to make them feel as bad as you feel or trying to make them change. Neither is a part of creating a healthy relationship. Rather than inviting a productive response from your partner, you're inviting anger.

How to Use "I" Statements" by Tony Robbins

https://bit.ly/4hrtGBB

An "I" statement, on the other hand, shows personal accountability. It states that even though your partner is not acting or speaking in the way you'd prefer, you are not blaming them for how you feel. When using "I" statements, you take responsibility for the part you played in the disagreement and display openness to deep listening and resolution.

"I" Statements by Therapist Aid

https://bit.ly/40NNyrt

When a person feels that they are being blamed—whether rightly or wrongly—it's common that they respond with defensiveness. "I" statements are a simple way of speaking that will help your clients avoid this trap by reducing feelings of blame. A good "I" statement takes responsibility for one's own feelings, while tactfully describing a problem.

"I Understand You Feel That Way, but I Feel This Way" References

https://bit.ly/4hOxcFX

Choosing the right words during an argument can be the difference between resolving your issues and making them worse. Make sure you communicate clearly. Avoid "you" statements. Switch to "I" or "we" and neutral language, especially when discussing difficult subjects.

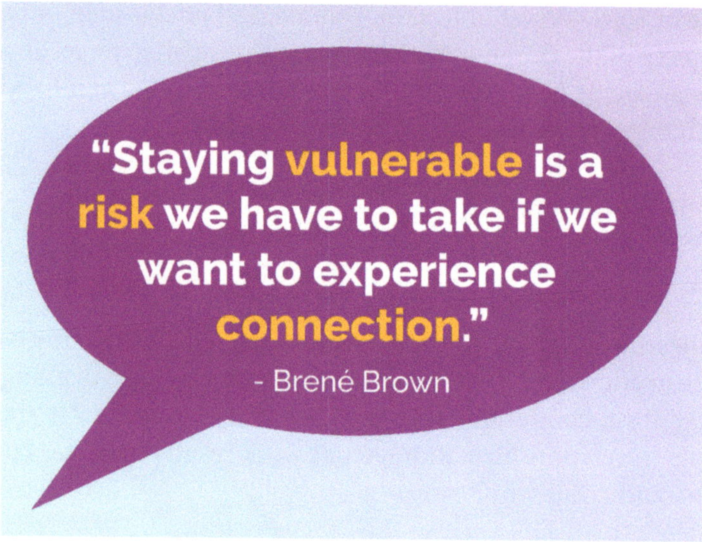

Instead of saying "You have a problem," try "What can we do together to improve [resolve, etc.]?"

In the spirit of clarity, it's better to explain (but not defend) yourself a little more than to potentially be misunderstood.

To avoid sounding accusatory or defensive, try shifting language from something like this:

"You know I care about you but what you did made me . . ."

And start your explanations with something more like this:

"From my perspective . . ."

"The way I understand it . . ."

"My experience of this situation was . . ."

If it sounds like you have to think ahead for how to express your thoughts, requests, and desires to someone you want to have a good outcome with, you are correct. Yes, it can feel like a lot of work, and maybe we can all look at the outcomes we live when we don't do the work! Full-blown arguments may occur, or silent distancing may escalate a situation to a place where each side feels badly, no effective listening is done, and no real solutions are achieved. The dinner table is strained at best and nonexistent at worst, bedtime is a battle, mornings are chaos, and the people we love the most are the ones we are most distant from.

I have worked with thousands of families and educators over the years, and whether the conversation was school- or family-related, the minute someone said, "You . . . ," the receiver felt personally affronted and defensive. I had tears in my office and in my home, as a professional and a mother. These tears were heartbreaking for all involved, and it does not have to be that way for you and your journey.

THE POWER OF "I" CAUTIOUS CONSIDERATIONS

While the Power of "I" is a beneficial tool for sharing, there are a few situations where using "I" can become misguided and manipulative in nature, even if not purposely meant to do so. It is important to understand that use of "I" inherently is not the tool. Use of "I" with the intent to connect, to understand, and to proactively self-express is the tool. Without these intentions, a misguided "I" statement can be followed by a "you" statement that becomes the overall message and can tear at trust and drive people away from us. A couple of cautions can keep the focus intentional and results more rewarding.

Caution #1: Blame and Guilt

Sometimes we may think that just putting an "I" in front of any statement creates the effect that we want. But this can be a clever way to place blame or guilt on the other person while claiming "good intent."

For example:

"I am frustrated when you don't do what you are supposed to do."

"I get tired of telling you the same thing over and over."

None of these have the likelihood of defusing the situation. Even though the sentences start with "I," they are still directing the blame outward and do not communicate your authentic feelings and needs while being responsible for them.

Here are few more examples with added underlying messages that are possible rather than the intended message:

"I told you I feel mad and unsupported when you don't help around the house, and you still don't help."

Underlying message:
"You don't care about me."

continued

continued from previous

This statement inherently sends a guilting message because it turns to finger-pointing. You can reframe it as follows:

"I feel unsupported when I don't have help around the house, and my reactions with you are snappy. I am curious what it will take for us to get on the same page so I can feel calm and happy and you can feel respected when I speak to you, even if we don't agree."

Underlying message:

"I care about how I treat you, I care about my well-being, and I care about solving a challenge I am having."

Caution #2: You Owe Me

Another caution is when "I" statements are messages of "owing" or "deserving" due to what one has done for another. Statements made from this mindset will not serve the goal of bridging differences and meeting needs. One way to look at this is to think about our own attitude toward what they owe us for doing X for them. There are times when parents feel their kids owe them for feeding them, for housing them, for giving them "things" and experiences. Something to consider, which may even be an "ouch" to recognize, is that unless we go into a transactional agreement with someone, no one owes us anything. When we have children or decide to teach, we decide to be in service to these amazing young humans. This does not mean we give up our entire life for them. There is a balance, of course, and to hold them responsible for some unknown reciprocity is unfair. Also to ask them to read our minds on what they "owe" us is unfair.

For example:

"I work so hard so you can have a good future. You don't appreciate anything I say or do for you."

The underlying message here combines both guilt and entitlement. What is missing is the speaker's accountability for choosing to work hard and choosing to offer the young person a brighter future. Also missing is an authentic request of need and agreement on expectations. This statement is likely to shut the listener down and escalate a power struggle.

Another "I" example that ultimately lands as a "you owe me" statement is this one:

"I call you all the time, but you never call me."

Underlying message:
"You are letting me down, and you don't care about me."

This can be transformed into a powerful "I" statement:

"I am missing you. I would love to hear from you more often, and I also know you are busy. It would mean a lot to me if we could connect more often, and I am wondering how we can make that happen."

Underlying message:
"I care about me, you, and us, so let's problem-solve."

Taking this a bit further, how do we use "I" when responses are not what we want? In the preceding examples, what if the person doesn't respond the way we want? What if we still don't have help around the house or a balanced friendship?

This is when we get to really pull on our SEL Muscles and elevate the use of our tool kit while also exploring our boundaries. At times, depending on the situation, the relationship, and the role of each person in the relationship, one must define a hard-line boundary. The SEL Muscles help us do this with assuredness while still being kind.

In the example about support around the house, let's assume there is no change after genuine effort to engage help. At this point, one might revert back to language that sounds like this:

"I try so hard, and you still haven't done anything to help me!"

Oops, that "I" is really a "you," and the statement is an invitation to a power struggle. Reflecting before slipping into this approach is important for everyone's sanity and well-being, starting with yours!

Questions for Reflection

What do I really want here?

What are my non-negotiables?

What am I willing to give up in order to have what I need?

Examples of this reflection might include the following:

What do I really want here?

- I want to feel seen, heard, and valued.
- I want to share the responsibility of life's general tasks; I don't want to go it alone.
- I want to have time for me and my interests and sanity.
- I want a space that feels cooperative and peaceful.

The Power of "I" Review

THE BASICS

- "I" statements focus on expressing personal feelings, needs, and experiences.
- They shift the dynamic from accusation to problem-solving.
- They develop accountability and acceptance.

WHY BOTHER?

- "I" statements reduce defensiveness and prevent power struggles.
- They build trust and credibility while maintaining respectful authority.
- They create productive communication and conflict resolution.

SECRET SAUCE

- Combine personal responsibility with proactive communication.
- Demonstrate vulnerability and humanity.
- Provide opportunities for "do-overs" to correct initial reactions.

AWESOME OUTCOMES

- Create atmospheres of "in it together" rather than "power over."
- Inspire mutually beneficial conversations and deeper relationships.
- Foster understanding and empathy between parties.

TIPS FOR SUCCESS

- **Model consistency:** Educators should consistently use "I" statements in their interactions with students, demonstrating how to express feelings and needs without blame. Parents should practice using "I" statements in everyday family conversations, even for minor issues, to normalize this communication style.
- **Acknowledge mistakes:** When educators or parents slip into using "you" statements, they should openly acknowledge it and ask for a "do-over" to rephrase using an "I" statement. This models accountability and shows young people that it's OK to make mistakes and try again.

- **Practice in low-stakes situations:** Educators can incorporate "I" statement practice into regular classroom activities, such as morning check-ins or group discussions. Parents can use family meetings or casual conversations as opportunities to encourage family members to express themselves using "I" statements, making it a natural part of family communication.

The Power of "I" Pause and Reflect

NOTICE.

- How do you feel, and what are your reactions when someone—a boss, family member, young person, or other person—starts a conversation with "*you* did," "*you* said," "*you* created," or "*you* made me"?
- Now consider how others who you have conflict with feel when they receive messaging in the same approach.

CHOOSE.

- What do you want to feel, and how do you want to react when in both easy and difficult conversations?
- How do you want to approach conversations and problem-solving? Be specific.

ACT.

- Identify two or three people you would like to have a closer, more trusted or productive relationship with.
- For each specific relationship and need you want to achieve better results from, identify specific "I" statements that will support proactive conversations and collaborative problem-solving.
- Consider possible obstacles to these actions and prethink a plan to overcome them.

Remember to use SEL Muscle #1, QTIP, while voicing feelings and needs, and be accountable for your words and actions.

MUSCLE #3

Ask vs. Tell

INTRODUCTION TO ASK VS. TELL

Muscle #3, Ask vs. Tell, is a nuanced articulation of identifying and asking for needs to be met. The approach of this SEL Muscle is to become focused on problem-solving rather than orienting toward complaint and accusation. Think about the typical dinner table or lunchroom at school. Are folks sharing good things or moaning about all that is wrong with all the "things" and all the "people"? Asking involves taking note of what is personally missing or doesn't feel good or safe in a situation, one that usually involves an upset. What does one need to turn the tables from upset to satisfaction? For those who care deeply about kids and others, which is presumably true of educators and carers, it can be really challenging to see within us because we are so often focused outside of us.

For instance, a teacher may need to ask for cooperation and understanding from students after a particularly challenging day while a mom might need support and to feel respect from her family to ease the burden of taking care of everyone while also working full-time. She might need more sleep to experience vitality. Humans tend to lean into complaint to garner what I call misery allies. There is truth in the adage "Misery loves company"! Ask vs. Tell helps shift us from misery-mining to joy cultivation by working collaboratively on solutions that feel good and productive rather than joining a pity party that seeks to keep an upset alive and, many times, thriving.

Ask vs. Tell is not simply asking for what we need—it is truly understanding what we need and then communicating it in a way where others can hear us, even if they don't agree with us. It is finding a way to communicate this (Muscles #1, QTIP, and #2, the Power of "I," come into play here) and feel secure in knowing we gave our best effort in taking care of ourselves regardless of the outcome. The good news is usually the outcome is much better than how we feel when we are drowning in the murky waters that come with complaining.

> **Watch out for the joy-stealers: gossip, criticism, complaining, fault-finding, and a negative, judgmental attitude.**
>
> - Joyce Meyer

ASK VS. TELL FOR EDUCATORS

Ask vs. Tell falls right in line with one of education's biggest focus areas, **growth mindset vs. fixed mindset**. Asking involves a growth mindset aptitude; telling involves a fixed mindset attitude. Notice that I used *aptitude* and *attitude*—this is purposeful. An aptitude is a skill, one we can work on and continue to grow in. An attitude is a belief that is often set and inflexible. A growth mindset allows us to consider, try, receive feedback, regroup, and try again. It is focused on forward movement even when there are setbacks. This is true for the *ask* part of Muscle #3. It is about considering what is needed from a genuine internal exploration followed by a carefully considered formulation of the spoken need. Telling aligns with a fixed mindset in that complaining makes everything other than one's opinion, upset, or desire wrong. When working in education environments, it is important to always remember we are in community and that in community there are many needs that are just as important as ours and that ours are just as important as theirs.

Asking, if thoughtful and genuine, in any form is an approach to collaborative problem-solving. This can be individual or with others. On the opposite side is telling, which inherently is about complaining about what is wrong in a situation or with another person(s), what is adversely affecting the "teller."

There are two distinct parts to the concept and use of Ask vs. Tell. Many of you may initially hear the title and jump to the thought that I am going to talk about asking others, especially our young folks, to do something rather than tell them to do it. This is a common concept in parenting programs and other communication styles. It has its place and can be really effective—when used intentionally and with thoughtful consideration. It is not, however, the core of what Ask vs. Tell is initially trying to accomplish.

Ask vs. Tell starts with looking deeper into ourselves and asking the first, and most important, question in all situations where an upset is brewing, has erupted, or needs cleanup. Feelings are hurt, and the path back to a mutually positive place is unclear and possibly even unwanted. In order to make significant progress in building rewarding relationships with both young people and colleagues, we will need to start identifying and asking for what we need in situations where an upset is happening or, better yet, what we need to keep an upset from ever beginning.

At this point, or somewhere in this reading, you may be thinking something like "I know what I need!"

I need rules to work:

- I need more cooperative students and parents and a supportive administration.
- I need viable consequences and reliable follow-through.
- I need policymakers who actually listen to those of us in trenches, and so on.

Basically, what we often think we need to be happy or successful are tangibles that other people control.

continued

continued from previous

- I need these kids to behave.
- I need administration to handle kids who are behavior challenges.
- I need policymakers to pass realistic legislation that helps me do my job.

All of this seems to make sense. So what is the challenge?

If we dive deeper and uncover the gnarly top layer that can be crusty and bitter because other people are not providing what we need, we may just find that what we need is about ourselves and our own well-being, regardless of all the other things we need others to do.

This is where we put the brakes on and redirect. What we are looking for (the *ask*) is not what we need others to do (the *tell*). It is about identifying what we are feeling and what we need to feel to be able to navigate our own emotions without flipping our lid. When we lose emotional control, it can create results that can be difficult to come back from.

Sometimes when I have lost control, it has definitely felt like I am having an adult temper tantrum. Over the years I have definitely had my turn at saying things I regret, been sulky and given the silent treatment, and even barked a harsh word or booted an item to make a point. None of these actions feel good to me or to others I care about. They are a result of me not finding a way to notice, and then articulate, what I was needing and what I was experiencing. Can you relate? Have there been times that you gave the silent treatment, yelled, whined, or stomped around so much that you noticed how awful you were acting but could not compose yourself?

As humans, we all have our moments and find ourselves behaving poorly in a variety of ways. Have you ever judged someone else's way of tempering only to realize that yours was equally ineffective, just different? That is one of those ouches I talk about. When we can look in the mirror and recognize our own meltdowns, we are starting the process of ownership and beginning to move closer to understanding the value of identifying, naming, and asking for what we need.

Here's an example of a teacher I worked with a long time ago and his aha *ask* moment:

Mr. Quest (name changed for privacy) was at his wit's end with several students in his history classes. History was Mr. Quest's jam: He loved everything about history and was passionate about his teaching. He was creative and gave students the opportunity to express their insights and learnings about history in a variety of ways. He was open to students' interpretations of history, and he valued robust dialogue about what he was teaching (to a point). In most educational settings he would be called a great teacher. However, there were those kids . . . the ones who derailed his brilliant teaching every day. He took this personally (Muscle #1), he blamed them for all the problems they created, he whined or barked about the time he was unable to teach (Muscle #2), and he spent every extra minute of his day complaining about the students and their parents and the administrators who did not support him.

The joy he felt in teaching was diminishing, and he blamed "those kids" and the system that did not have his back. He did ask for help; however, the asking was always about how the other person could "deal" with those kids, not how he could reach them in a different way. When Mr. Quest and I met for the third time so he could tell me how poorly they were doing and how they continued to be disrespectful and defiant, I decided to approach him in a new way. I asked him what he needed. He started with the long list of what he needed from others. I carefully and respectfully redirected the question, asking him what he needed to feel fulfilled in his job. This stopped him, and he became quiet. It took a beat, but he finally answered,

"I need to make sure students understand the value and importance of history. When people don't understand, history will repeat itself, and terrible things from the past are likely to happen again."

Mr. Quest was worried about the future. He worried and cared deeply about the lives of those whom he taught. He worried that if these students—all students—didn't "get" history, they might live a more difficult life. Mr. Quest's upset originated in a desire to serve, and these students had no idea. They only heard him rail on them. Berate them. Not believe in them.

Once we got to this awareness, we talked about a new way to approach these students—a new way to communicate with them. We also talked about how unwilling he'd been to allow students to have differing passions and interests from his, to not see history as he did. He was a great teacher, and he knew it. In that knowing he also had blinders on, blinders that prevented him from "seeing" each young person's potential regardless of their shared interest.

continued

continued from previous

Mr. Quest ultimately had a private conversation with each student. He was able to express how frustrated he'd been feeling because he really was committed to a future that was safe and enjoyable for them and for all people. He shared that he understood that they didn't necessarily see history through the same lens as him, and he asked them what ignited their passion as history did his. He shared what he needed from them: Even if they didn't love his class, he still needed their cooperation. Then he asked them what he could count on from them.

In the end Mr. Quest's relationship with all but one of these students dramatically improved. They still were not interested in history, but the parties became interested in each other and had a desire to show respect and ask more questions and reveal more feelings. It was a success story that Mr. Quest could not see before he gave Ask vs. Tell a try and flexed his SEL Muscles.

Ask vs. Tell is incredibly effective in relationships of all kinds. Once we have figured out the first step, identifying needs and feelings, it is time to formulate it into the actual ask. The formation of an ask takes multiple things into consideration.

Is it an ask or an expectation? We all have experienced the different feelings of being told by a boss, a colleague, or another person what to do or otherwise being asked to do something, but it wasn't really an ask; it was a requirement stated as an ask. It is important to be clear in our communication that what we are saying is meeting our expectations. For instance:

"Would you please take out your journals and begin responding to the prompt on the board?'"

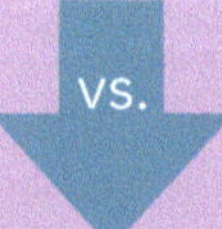

"Next we are going to take out our journals and begin responding to the prompt on the board. Please complete this by 8:30—that's 10 minutes from now."

The first is a request, and students or others have the space to decline because it is a request. The second is an expectation that is clear and has defined requirements. To manage asking in an effective way it is important to choose our words carefully and clearly. We also need to be responsible for accepting a decline when what we have "asked" really only has one answer in our mind.

Am I asking someone to guess exactly what I mean or read my mind?

"Next time try harder, and you will do better on the next test."

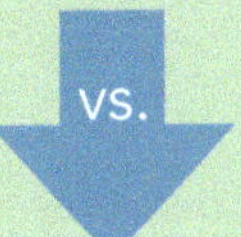

"I see that you struggled with this test. I feel concerned, and I imagine it feels bad to you. I wonder if we could work together and make a plan that will set you up for better results next time. Would you be interested in that?"

Let's deconstruct these statements. The first one is a *tell*. There is no asking for anything. Also, it assumes something that is very common in education, that a student knows exactly what certain things mean and how to execute them. For a struggling student, telling them to "try harder," "study more," or "pay attention" may sound good and have no effect because they simply do not know how. Or know where to start. Or understand what strategies are available to them for support.

One of the most impactful interactions I had with a teacher was in my first year of community college. I recall her now as I can see how she approached me in the nature of *asking*, and it made a huge difference in my school career and future successes.

I was taking a dreaded math class. Math always felt like a nemesis; it was against me, and often it won the battle and left me in tears and escalating insecurities. This was a required class, and I was lost. I did or attempted all of my homework, I studied, and I stressed. None of that actually seemed to help me.

One day, as we sat to take an exam, I found myself staring at questions that I had no idea how to answer. I sat for minutes in a complete panic and growing despair—I could not fail this class; it was the gateway to my future career. I was quiet, reserved, and insecure, and this moment did not help at all. After fretting for too long and answering no questions, I finally pulled on some deeply hidden courage and took my test to the teacher at the front of the room.

Me: **"I am sorry, but I can't take this test. I know I will fail. I really do not understand it at all."**

Teacher: **Reaching for the untouched test I had in my hand and looking at me directly, kindly, inquisitively, "Why would I have you take a test you know you will fail? That would make no sense. Why don't you go get your book and come sit here with me, and I'll help you? Once you are ready, we will arrange for you to take the test."**

Without a doubt this teacher (regretfully I do not recall her name) changed the course of my school career. She was instrumental in building my confidence and my willingness to trust approaching a teacher for help. I had had other great teachers, but only a few made such an indelible impression and lifelong impact, and this was in college! I sometimes wonder how great it would have been for me to start building confidence much earlier—I am sure this question is answered in the work I develop.

As a culture, we typically frame and reward the models of *do* and *telling*. We often value task accomplishment more than relationship-building. Yet anyone who is in a relationship with young people knows that they generally follow your guidance more when they have a positive relationship with you, particularly as they grow older. Effective asking can enhance your credibility in terms of relationship-building, as you are expressing authentically about yourself and are genuinely curious about them, their behaviors and choices, and how to guide them strategically.

Effective asking can make other people feel comfortable and disarm any defensiveness that might arise if they were ordered to do something instead, even if the same request is being couched in a question. Effective asking can reveal what is important to a young person so that you can see what to leverage most productively. Effective asking can cause a young person to think about what you want them to think about without them feeling manipulated or made wrong. You ask the questions in ways that invite the exchanges, valuing the input of others, which is what everyone needs to be more willing to listen, learn, shift, agree, and at times even acquiesce.

Asking is a combination of tapping into what we need and being able to voice it in a way that is disarming. You could say "I need you to be quiet!," but what is the underlying need in that statement? The underlying need could be that you need to feel successful at teaching a lesson, you need to feel respected and heard, or you need to feel productive as an educator. So, if you can find ways to voice that without pointing fingers at your students for the ways that they are hindering your wishes, you'll find more open students who demonstrate a willingness and desire to meet your needs.

Also, *telling* is often relatively synonymous with complaining or trying to get someone else in trouble. Think of children when they're young. "I'm telling!" slips easily out of their mouths, always in an effort to report the bad behavior of someone else. But when we ask, we're asking for support, whether it is for ourselves or for someone else. When asking, we are in a problem-solving mindset. When I ask, I'm requesting collaborative problem-solving rather than telling others what is "wrong."

USING MUSCLES #1, #2, AND #3 TOGETHER

The first three SEL Muscles build upon each other and can be incredibly effective when used together. The following dialogue uses components of all three to address a challenge and request a collaborative resolution.

Teacher: **Good morning, how are we all today?**

[Pause and let them answer.]

Teacher: **My morning has been unusually challenging. I had very little sleep last night, and everything seemed to go wrong this morning. Now I am feeling more edgy and impatient than usual, and I am not a fan of myself when I act like this with you. Has anyone else ever had one of those mornings?**

[The question is generally rhetorical and designed to get buy-in and engagement from your students.]

Teacher: **It may take me a beat to reset and get back to my normal self. I would like to ask for your extra cooperation this morning and your patience. I promise I am doing my best to rebound quickly. Can I count on this from all of you? If not, could you please share with me what I can count on? I would appreciate knowing that.**

Our students do have hearts, and when they see you as multidimensional and potentially even vulnerable in similar ways to them, they will be more likely to fulfill your requests. In fact, they are likely to go out of their way to make sure they are making things easier for you.

As adults, it may be challenging at times to choose to focus on the solution, rather than the problem. It is often faster to address the problem, and typically autopilot takes over and we don't even think about it when we start down the path of complaint. This, however, can erode relationships and our positive sense of self. Ideally, you are understanding what you need and how it makes you respond, and then wrapping it into a request to solve it. You are offering that you can be a part of the solution, and so can your students. Then, even if they still do not honor your request, you can feel good about yourself because at least you tried, even if the outcome wasn't what you would have liked. Some days that may be the most that you can accomplish, and that is OK. It can still be enough to preserve your mental health and allow you to come back the next day, ready to enjoy the task of reaching and teaching your students again. Does it work every time? Nothing works every time! But it does chip away at what is not working.

ASK VS. TELL FOR FAMILIES AND CARERS

Ask vs. Tell has much overlap in how to use it in families with how it is used by educators. The recognition of why it is a powerful and useful SEL Muscle in the home is a bit different philosophically, and uncovering the layers is critical for those of us raising young people. The key for all of us is to keep in mind that Ask vs. Tell is about identifying needs and feelings and creating a space for them to be met or at least addressed.

As parents and carers raising young people, we are often moving so fast from event to event, task to task, obligation to obligation, that we can find ourselves depleted and cranky before we ever even notice that we haven't taken a moment for ourselves. We might find ourselves withering into an abyss that we don't see coming, and our response to this is a version of ourselves that is often impatient, rigid, exhausted, short-tempered, whiny, or a myriad of other behaviors.

In all the hussle, what we imagine we are creating is a full and optimal life for our young people; however, often what we are missing in the equation of raising children is ourselves and our needs. Of course, there is a balancing act between providing a safe and healthy childhood for our children and making sure we don't lose ourselves in the process. When we had children, we inherently gave up a 100% "about me" mindset. We decided to share our lives in service to raising our children. Often, however, we go too far away from ourselves in the process.

It is important to remember that this is our lifetime too, that every breath we take is a gift and it is not guaranteed. In trainings I often ask,

> "How many of you in this room know someone who did not get enough days?"

This is a heavy and humbling question. Invariably almost everyone raises their hand, and if it is a crowd of folks over 30, it seems everyone raises their hand. We do not know how long we will have on this planet, and it is up to us to create a life that

- **we feel proud of,**
- **fulfills us, and**
- **models what we hope for our young people.**

Candidly, when I was raising my own kids, I was not aware of my lack of attention to these parts of myself. I did not know how to ask for what I needed because I didn't even know to look for what I needed. My focus was solely on providing for my children—on giving them every opportunity and scrambling to "fix" any and all things that seemed, to me, less than optimal.

Until I was about 40 I am not sure I ever even questioned what I needed or what I was deeply feeling. Funny thing is that as a school counselor I was teaching this stuff to other parents, and youth, but blinded from seeing it for myself. I thought I had it under control—**until my own kids showed me otherwise**.

The journey of discovering what I needed was not an easy one, and the relationship I had with my children was compromised as they became more aware than I was. The impact of not knowing or asking for what I needed created a model for my children that was challenging for them to make sense of. They could see through the illusion I had wrapped myself in, that all was well with me when it really wasn't.

My children, all of our children, have built-in hypocrisy radars, and when we say things that they can see are not true, it messes with their own sense of self. The best gift we can give our children is to be true to ourselves. The way to do this is to identify our feelings and not only ask for what we need but also ask them what they need. Help them learn to identify what is emoting inside of them and then teach them to honor and manage these feelings in healthy and productive ways. The first step to achieve this is doing it ourselves so they see it in productive and healthy action. Even when we get it wrong, we can be assured they are learning and developing strong skills in resilience and agency as they witness us ***recognize***, ***recover***, and ***reengage***.

LET'S LOOK AT HOW ASK VS. TELL PLAYS OUT IN THE 3 *R*s

Recognize: Notice what is happening and ask yourself how you truly feel about it. Notice if you are ignoring it, brushing it aside or under the proverbial rug, or addressing it head-on. Notice your attitudes, words, and actions around it. Is it more like the *tell* attitude—complaining, feeling victimized, blaming others? Or is it framed more as an *ask* aptitude—what do I need, what is missing, how are my feelings driving my attitudes and actions?

Recover: Consider options, choose purposely to proactively honor what you are needing, and voice it in appropriate and helpful ways. Maybe you need to ask for support from others, and maybe you need to take time for yourself. Maybe you need to ask someone you trust to be a listening ear who will let you vent it off and then support you in productive next steps.

Reengage: This is where action happens—where we say the words, ask the questions, and take the steps needed to try again. This is where resiliency shows up. Before reengagement, resilience is simply an idea.

A FEW EXAMPLES

Mornings are hectic, even chaotic, as you try to get yourself and your kids ready for a new day of work, school, afternoon activities, homework, meal prep, and so on. You are up early, after having not slept enough, to be sure all the things get done. You wake up your kids—5 times before they get out of bed; you prep breakfast—which is met with complaint that it is not the right breakfast; you tell your kids to get their school stuff together and get it in the car—which one of them doesn't do, and you don't realize this until after you've left the house. You realize that teeth aren't brushed and beds aren't made but decide you can only take on so many battles so you ignore it along with the cold cup of coffee you poured an hour ago and never took a sip of. You grin and bear it all, then kiss the kids goodbye as you drop them at school and hustle off to work. Maybe after you settle more into your day you reflect on how short you were with the kids, how grumpy and exhausted you were, and how that affected your mood even though you tried for it not to. Maybe you never even look at this because you wrap yourself in this story:

Your kids are good, and you are good, because the "things" got done. But really, are you good? What could make this better? What can you identify in feelings and needs that would make it so you could peacefully drink a hot cup of coffee or have a shower that doesn't need to happen an hour before you wake up the kids, leaving you sleep deprived? What could you share and ask for that would build agency in the family, individually and collectively, while providing ease and grace for you? What could happen that would calm your nervous system, and theirs?

What can you do so you don't diminish your power by going down the path of complaining or, maybe even worse, pretending all is fine? Remember the only person believing you are fine is you. Everyone else sees through you, and it hurts them. I totally learned this the hard way.

Here are a few thoughts for you to consider sharing with your family. First create a space where your family can "hear" you in a new and different way. They are used to hearing you tell them all that is wrong with the chaotic mornings and what you want them to do differently even though it doesn't typically change anything for long.

Ideas for creating a new space of sharing: Create something random and unexpected that they will question but not hate (except the part where they're not allowed to use their devices, which needs to be the case for you, too, in all these examples).

- Have a carpet picnic for dinner, or go to the park and have dinner.
- Call a family huddle around a shared dessert or other treat.
- Take a walk, hike, or drive with everyone.
- Create an atmosphere that is calm and warm—different.

Once you are in a new and different atmosphere and your family is a bit uneasy simply because it is so new, open a conversation. Here is an entry point for you to consider:

> **"I am happy to be having this time together. I have something I would like to share, and then I am hoping to hear from you as well. I have realized recently that I am often cranky, exhausted, and on edge. I am not pleasant to be around. My patience is stretched, and the way I speak to you all is not always kind or loving. I don't like this about myself, and I am guessing you don't like it about me either.**
>
> [At this point you have their attention.]
>
> **I have made a new commitment to myself and to you all: I am going to focus on being my happy self, and that means I need to take care of myself more so I can feel calmer and balanced. What I need is for us to make a plan together that will help me achieve this goal. Each of us has an important role in our own life and in our family life.**

continued

continued from previous

Then, check in with them:

What are you thinking? What questions do you have for me?

Continue from here in making a plan that increases agency for each person and eases the burden for you. Some examples that work wonders:

- Each person gets an old-school alarm clock that gets set, and each person is responsible for getting themselves up and out of bed each day. (Keep this age-appropriate of course; I use this technique with students in kindergarten and up.)
- Each person gets themselves dressed, sometimes setting clothes out the night before.
- Parents are responsible for their own care while young people are responsible for theirs.
- Parents are waiting in the kitchen—having their morning beverage or other routine—when kids arrive ready for breakfast.

One parent I worked with who had 6-year-old twins was absolutely shocked at how well all this worked. Her twins went from causing morning chaos that was like having the Tasmanian devil × 2 in her home every morning to having them join her for breakfast after handling *all* their own stuff. She literally told the parenting group I was coaching, "I actually had a quiet cup of hot coffee every morning last week!"

Notice how in this scenario (a real one) the parent used "I" statements (Muscle #2), was not angry or finger-pointing about all that "they" were doing (Muscle #1, QTIP), and asked for what she was needing without feeling shame or guilt. She asked for a collaborative approach: Let's make a plan together. There was no option that there needed to be a plan, but there was a consideration that everyone could be a part of it.

ASK VS. TELL AS A POWERFUL GAME-CHANGER

Like the other SEL Muscles, Ask vs. Tell needs to be routinely flexed to keep it strong. Remember that we all have setbacks to our SEL Muscle development, and just like everything else, practice makes us stronger and getting positive results easier and more successful.

CAUTIOUS CONSIDERATIONS

Ask vs. Tell is a powerful tool when used to explore and share feelings and needs with others. Asking humanizes and builds trust. There are, however, a couple cautions to be aware of to be sure this SEL Muscle is being flexed both correctly and effectively.

Caution #1: Are We Really Asking?

The most common misconception about Ask vs. Tell is that we should ask others to do what we want rather than tell them to. For example:

"Would you please take out your homework and turn it in?"

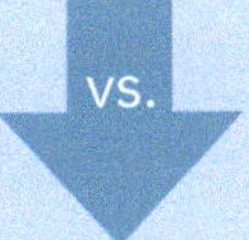

"Take out your homework and put it in the tray.'"

or

"Will you please take out the trash?"

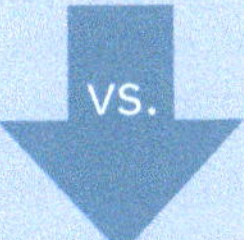

"Take the trash out."

While these are important distinctions in how we communicate with others, the difference is mostly about being courteous. Overall, most people respond better to people who are courteous and respectful. It is important when flexing Muscle #3 that you are distinguishing what you need as a part of the ask, not just politely asking someone to do something. Adding to the previous examples, one can take the polite ask and reframe it in a way that might address your needs as well as your request.

For example:

"I am excited for us to get started today. If you have your homework, please put it in the tray. That will help me have more time to support those of you who have questions about the homework."

This statement wraps your needs into the request and shares a bit about what you are feeling at the moment. There is enthusiasm in the request and an invitation for students to not have it perfectly all together.

"I am feeling exhausted and overwhelmed at the moment. I need support to get my day done so I can rest and be in a better mood. I'm sure we'd both be happy about that! While I work on dinner, can I count on you taking out the trash before we eat?"

This request acknowledges you, your feelings, your needs, and the other person. It is framed in a way that is respectful of both parties. It is important that you make sure the other person offers a response to your request—this is how accountability is established and measured and another way trust is built.

Caution #2: Guilt and Shame

The second caution looks at the need for us to be certain we are not leveraging our feelings to elicit a desired response through guilt or shaming. Like in Muscle #2, the Power of "I," we can say the words in such a way that what is received on the other end is a message that is meant to convey a "don't let me down" or "you owe me" type of message, a *tell.*

For example:

"I feel so disappointed. After all the time I have spent trying to help you pass this class, why can't you just get your homework done?"

This comment uses an "I" statement, and it formulates a question; however, the underlying message is more of a "you" statement:

"I've gone out of my way to help you, and you owe me some return. I am disappointed in you!"

If accountability and trust-building was the intention, an ask such as this could be better formulated:

"I am feeling uncertain on the best way to support you. I want you to do well, and I would like to know what you want. It seems that when we work together, you make progress, but when you are expected to work independently, like on homework, you are having a hard time. Can we talk about what you need and make a plan for your success together?"

Here is an example for parents and carers:

"You are old enough to do some chores around the house, I don't ask much of you, it is not that hard, and I am tired of asking you, over and over every day, why don't you just do what I ask?"

This response starts with you and is already off to a challenging start. The adult says, "I am tired of." While "tired" can be a feeling, in this case it is a complaint. There is a question, "why don't you just," but it is really a shaming statement, a judgment that has very little chance of gaining meaningful attention or developing any social-emotional agency. What might have more chance of creating a positive outcome is an ask such as this:

"I realized lately that I've been resentful and unhappy when I come home and basic chores are not done. I find myself barking or practically begging for help. I do not like this about myself. What I need is for us to make a plan where all of us can contribute to the house regularly so all of us, including me, can have more time for doing the things that make us happy."

This response takes ownership of feelings and of the consequences that result from them. It makes a fair and reasonable request that demonstrates the carer's value and worth. It clearly details what is needed while giving the others voice in contributing to the plan. From here the conversation has many opportunities for sharing and creating a plan that supports the ask.

Ask vs. Tell Review

THE BASICS

- Ask vs. Tell shifts focus from complaint and accusation to problem-solving.
- Asking involves self-reflection and clarification of needs.
- Ask vs. Tell is the difference between a growth mindset and a fixed mindset.

WHY BOTHER?

- Building bridges gets you farther than misery allies ever will.
- Asking cultivates joy by creating actionable solutions. Misery-mining keeps the problem alive.
- Communicating needs effectively transforms relationships.

SECRET SAUCE

- Ask, "What do I really need?," and then express it in a way others can hear.
- Approach your needs with curiosity and openness and be ready to adjust and try again.
- Notice your words, tones, moods, and attitudes and, when needed, pivot.

AWESOME OUTCOMES

- **For educators:** Fosters a classroom culture that invites dialogue and collaboration between teacher and students and students and students. Develops agency and understanding.
- **For parents:** Creates more harmony, connection and conversation with all family members. Develops independence and empathy.
- Promotes problem solving over complaining.

TIPS FOR SUCCESS

- **Try new questions:** Rather than declaring something is wrong with them (e.g., "You are being ridiculous—knock it off!") or minimizing with a "What's wrong?," ask, instead, "What's going on for you right now?" or "What do you need right now?"
- **Seek collaboration:** Lean into problem-solving approaches, asking, "What would help make this easier?," instead of simply demanding compliance or giving in.
- **Identify and ask:** Remember yourself as a part of the equation and ask for what you need with respect rather than falling into blame or criticism.

Ask vs. Tell Pause and Reflect

NOTICE.

- Do you usually *ask* or *tell* when something is missing or needing to be fixed?
- Do you usually achieve the results you hope for easily and without upsetting yourself or others?
- What feelings and behaviors do you experience when *asking* (or *telling*) does not go well or easily?
- What are a few areas (personal, career, caretaking, relationships) in your life where you are not thriving, not feeling like you are at the top of your game or having the relationship you want?
- How do you feel in each of them?
- What behaviors are you engaging in, perhaps that you may not feel good about?

CHOOSE.

- In each area you identified, what do you want instead?
- How do you want to be feeling? What behaviors will follow if you feel the way you want to?
- What kind of conversations do you want to have?
- What do you want others to know about you and what you need so you can live full-out, mattering as much as everyone around you, with joy and ease?

ACT.

- List specific conversations you are going to have that will include the first three SEL Muscles:
  - **QTIP:** What specifically are you not taking personally even if it would be easy to do so?
  - **The Power of "I":** How will you frame your *ask* using an "I" statement?
  - **Ask vs. Tell:** How will you ask for what you need and avoid complaining? How are you being intentional about being proactive and coming from a place of problem-solving?
- When will you have these conversations? What obstacles might get in the way of having these conversations, and what can you do to avoid or overcome them?

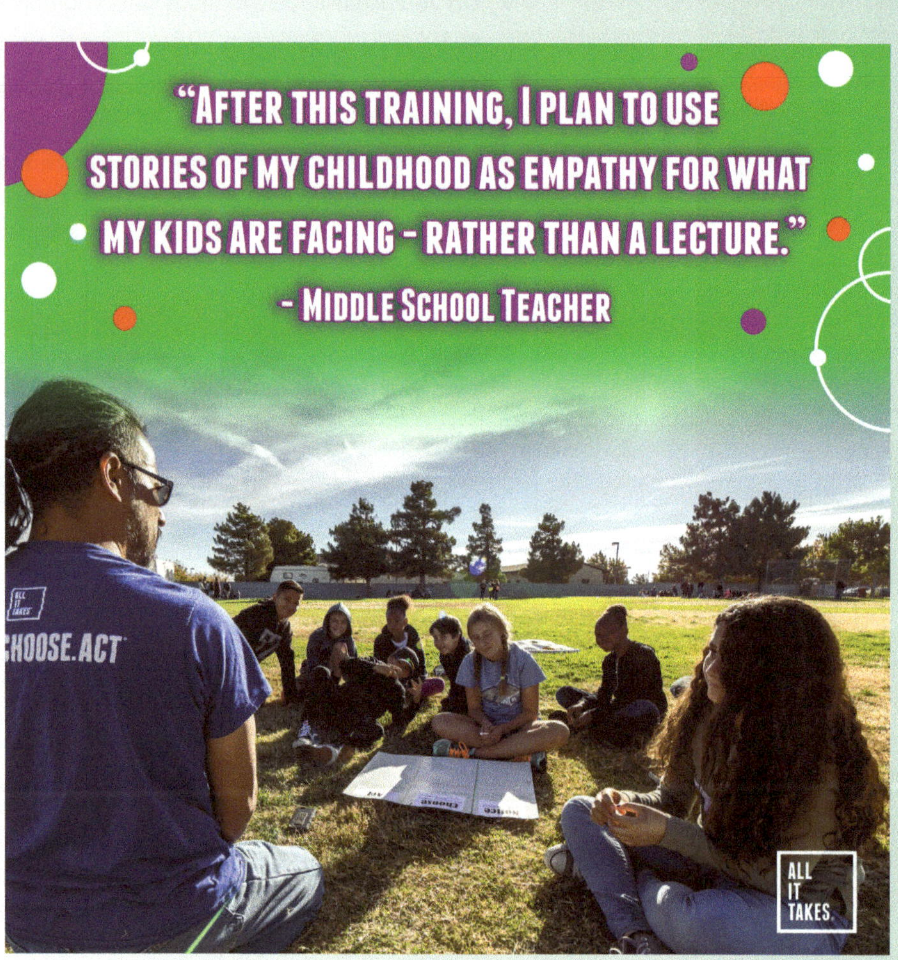
"After this training, I plan to use
stories of my childhood as empathy for what
my kids are facing - rather than a lecture."
- Middle School Teacher
CHOOSE.ACT
ALL
IT
TAKES.

MUSCLE #4

Storytelling

INTRODUCTION TO STORYTELLING

Storytelling is one of the most powerful and effective ways to deliver a message. It has sacred origins and is a treasured way of communicating among Indigenous nations around the world. It is one of the first ways we are taught how to listen and learn as a human. Storytelling is used in many aspects of our life from bedtime stories to a grandparent's tale around the dinner table or while sitting on a lap and of course as a messaging tool in elementary school up through college. Storytelling is a creative and effective way for material to reach an audience. And the impact of storytelling can stretch far beyond the original walls in which it was shared.

This SEL Muscle has a specific nature that distinguishes it from other forms of storytelling. Some forms of storytelling are meant to purely entertain, spinning

grand tales created out of endless imagination that captivates and inspires, gripping audiences throughout the ages. The focus of Muscle #4 is on using storytelling to relate, to build bridges and create trust. Storytelling in this way uses personal experiences and feelings to relate to another's feelings even if the experiences are completely different such as intergenerational understanding and intercommunity culture.

STORYTELLING FOR EDUCATORS

Why Do We Tell Stories?

Whether in caves or in cities, storytelling remains the most innate and important form of communication. All of us tell stories—the story of your day, the story of your life, workplace gossip, the horrors on the news. Our brains are hardwired to think and express in terms of a beginning, middle, and end. It's how we understand the world. **Storytelling is the oldest form of teaching.** It bonded the early human communities, giving children the answers to the biggest questions of creation, life, and the afterlife. Stories define us, shape us, control us, and make us. Not every human culture in the world is literate, but every single culture tells stories.

As educators, why do we tell stories—especially our (age-appropriate) personal stories—to the young people we serve? And are we maximizing the tool that stories can be?

Let me explain: Stories have the great power and opportunity to help people not feel alone in their experiences and feelings. Educators telling stories can tell them to teach or tell them to relate. Telling stories to relate brings our young people toward us while telling stories to teach or persuade can create greater distance between us. They can see what our underlying message is (be more appreciative, work harder, stop doing this or that, etc.) and will often be inclined to disregard any value that we were trying to impart with our story, feeling misunderstood and disenchanted.

When a story is being told, it usually has an underlying message or lesson that the speaker is trying to convey to the audience. Storytelling, when used well, can be an excellent tool. It helps explain expectations, strengthen character, and teach desired behavior within a particular setting. When a speaker turns information into a relatable story with a lesson attached, it's easier for the audience to connect to and learn from it. Stories make people want to listen, by taking an abstract theory and turning it into a story with an emotional plot. From a teaching perspective, sharing important information through a storyline will engage your students. It will also increase your chances of being not only heard but thoroughly understood.

Whether you fail or succeed, you still walk away from every situation with a story to tell that ends with a lesson you learned. When you inform your young people about something that they can relate to based on actual events in their life experience, you are creating a mutual understanding that can deepen the lesson and improve its chances of retention and impact.

For educators, the main thing to remember is that we are rewarded when we tell stories to relate and not to teach or convince! Sometimes we may be able to slip our message into our stories, but that should not be the focus. If we want our students to grow with us, to trust us, and to learn from us, we need to tell stories that are inspiring, relatable, and meant to create more understanding. Stories are ideal when they make our students feel understood.

Our young people's lives do have many differences from our own, but in essence many of the feelings are similar. We don't need to meet them in a shared experience through our storytelling, but we do want to meet them in shared feelings.

WHAT TO KEEP IN MIND

Once you decide to expand or implement storytelling into your classroom or program, make sure to keep the following things in mind to ensure the highest level of impact for your students:

- The stories you tell should be short and to the point. This helps keep the audience's attention. If your story is too long, then there's a greater possibility that your audience will lose interest. So make it short, sweet, and to the point *or* the most engaging story that has your young audience sitting on the edge of their chairs, hanging on every word. There are some people who are natural orators and can tell a riveting story. This is not a requirement, however, to create relatedness with your young people. What is most important is that you are authentically yourself. Your audience will care about your genuineness more than your entertainment value—as long as you remember the story is for them, not yourself.
- The stories you tell should be easy to understand so the speaker's message doesn't get lost. If you use big words or complicated storylines, it will be easy for the listener to get confused and stop listening. So make it an easy and enjoyable listen.
- The stories you tell should spark emotion and be relatable for your audience. If a story is significant to you, it will show in your delivery and then become significant to your audience as well. So make emotion a priority.
- The stories you tell should have a final lesson at the end that ties in your original message. If your initial thought is clear at the end of your story, then your audience will take away more from the experience. So make sure your message creates good follow-through and takeaways.

A story doesn't have to be elaborate to be heard and remembered. It takes a good plot, a good lesson, and to be told in a way that its intended audience can hear the message, without defensiveness.

Storytelling is a powerful method of communication. It offers people the opportunity to connect to, relate to, or see the world from someone else's perspective. Stories provoke our emotions. They can make us laugh, cry, feel afraid, get angry, think, and dream. Following a character on a journey of exploration, empathizing with the character's problem, yearning for a solution, and reveling in the outcome help to shape our mental state.

These days, with the uncanny pace of technology, slang, trends, and all the things that rapidly change and that we often cannot relate to, we must work to connect with the feelings of our stories. We must look for the parallels between the emotions and the challenges and even reflections from our lives that are relatable, whether we know them from pop culture, social media, or anyplace that doesn't violate the privacy of the original storyteller. This can also be a good lesson in when and how we share other people's stories.

WHAT IS THE MAIN OBJECTIVE OF ANY STORYTELLING?

In our work and relationships with young people, the goal is to connect with them. The teachable moments or messages imparted are secondary to the connection that you are creating. The goal is for the students and young people to see you more as a human, and, wise little beings that they are, they know when you are trying to authentically connect with them rather than judging, which places more distance between their human experience and yours.

HOW DO WE KNOW WHAT STORIES TO TELL?

Do we have a few stock stories on deck, or do we pull them out of a proverbial hat when the need arises and triggers the memory of a *correlative* story in our brain? Do the stories have to be true?

How to Be Best Prepared

For an educator, there will be lessons that you must repeat at different times. Having a few *stock* stories that relate well to the subject at hand is a good idea. Just like a comedian tries out new material or a chef plays with recipes, you can try different stories and see what works. You must also still have the awareness that what worked once may not work again in a different situation or with a different audience.

Of course, as an educator, you know the value and skill of style flexing! Be on your toes about how to adjust your approach and strategies for different kids, or even the same kids on a different day!

Think of stories that draw you into them. Think of some people who are powerful storytellers; this could be writers, artists, musicians, a neighbor, someone bagging your groceries for you, a fellow educator, or anyone! What do others do to engage you and encourage you to keep listening, keep reading, keep watching, buy a product, laugh, or follow a social media page—all the things?!

Try to see what the underlying factors are that make them appealing. For most people authenticity ranks quite high on our list of what we connect with. I know some of the new "famous people" may belie that a bit, but actually they're also falling for a story—a story of fantasy life, filtered life, a curated life—when in reality, of course, there are many layers behind those curated images and stories.

With the emergence of artificial intelligence (AI), I feel that people are more than ever trying to determine what is real. And what is often missing from overly synthesized music or AI text is the clear touch of a human. It is even an almost indefinable thing, but I believe that our young people are still better at detecting what is real than anyone older. They are feeling creatures and have not yet built up the walls that we adults have in the ways that we process and interpret information, generally making us more thought- and action-oriented than feelings-oriented.

And, of course, our young people are wondering: What is real? They stand on shakier ground in terms of having to discern from such a young age what is real and what is not. Our kids want connection in the way that it felt having a bedtime story read to them, or having someone show up to watch their game or performance, or receiving an encouraging text from their best friend. They want to be held, and they want to be seen. Most of them would never say it and truly may not even be fully aware that it is the feeling they're after. They crave connection, and stories can be a wonderful bridge to create it.

Of course, some people love to tell stories. We probably all know someone who can make a dramatic story about going to the post office. But if you are not a regular storyteller, and you feel as though it is not a comfort zone to you, then remember that we're not telling stories for dramatic effect. We're not telling them to be as original or compelling as possible. We're telling them to connect with our students. That is the primary objective. So it could be as simple as this:

"When I was your age, I had a teacher who I felt never understood me. I wasn't doing well in the class, and I felt like he couldn't see when I was actually trying but still didn't understand the material. I felt like he only saw me as a problem or a bad grade. When I became a teacher myself, I planned to always try to understand where my students are coming from. I try to remember that what I see of you is just the tip of the iceberg for all that is going on with you. I want to know what you are thinking and feeling so that I can truly help. Have any of you ever felt misunderstood like I did? What was that like for you?"

It's not a dramatic story; it doesn't have a punchline, climax, or compelling storyline. It is just a simple reminder that you were once a student struggling to learn, too, and wishing that your teacher could see that and understand you.

So don't be daunted by the word *storytelling*. Throw away the idea that you need dramatic descriptions, a narrative arc, or anything that detailed. All you need is a desire to create some cord of connection and relatability with your student(s). Ideally, they will resonate with that feeling, even if they don't resonate with the story you told.

Flex for Success

If you're stepping into a gym for the first time ever, you're not going to go directly to the heavy weightlifting section. Many of us never will! You'll start small and begin building your muscles. You'll embrace repetition and push yourself further when you feel ready. For years I felt self-conscious of storytelling, measuring my self-perceived shortcomings against who I labeled as expert storytellers. For a long time, this self-imposed critique stopped me from trying. Once I decided to flex this SEL Muscle and be honest and authentic, I saw firsthand how audiences reacted and leaned in, and it was one of the greatest gifts I gave myself. If you're not used to sharing stories with your students, give yourself grace and tread lightly; go slowly yet purposefully. And if stories don't "land" with your students, practice Muscle #1, QTIP, and try a new one another day. As you know, we can have what feels like the best-laid plans and the most engaging content, and sometimes we can barely get our students to stop texting during class. Refrain from judging yourself, or them, for not connecting with your story. Flex this SEL Muscle again when you feel ready; as we tell our students, success comes with practice.

What If Storytelling Is Not Your Thing?

Keep in mind that you can always use stories that are not your own but are still real and meaningful to you. Like I shared, storytelling was a challenging SEL Muscle for me to learn to flex; I always felt insecure and often struggled to "lighten up." What worked best for me was just jumping in and building on my "being vulnerable" skills. Other ways are to practice telling stories to a friend, a spouse, or another young person in your life who is not a student of yours. Ask for feedback and laugh about it if that feels comfortable.

For example, you tell your teenage niece a story and ask if she thinks that other teenagers can relate to it. Tell your friend a story you chose specifically for them and see if they light up and can resonate with it. Become familiar with the *connection* aspect of it. Often, even when I check out at a grocery store, I try to connect with the person who's ringing up my groceries (not always, as we all have times when we're not up for conversation!).

When they ask, "How's your day going?" I offer more than the requisite "Fine" or something similar. I respond with something really going on for me and then ask them about them.

"I was late this morning, and it set my whole day off on the wrong foot."

"I'm buying this ice cream to eat with a friend tonight who is going through a hard time."

It can be literally anything! When I leave, I aim to feel like we had a brief but real human connection, and hopefully I made their day a little more entertained. Hopefully I made them feel that I see their human-ness and let them into mine as well.

I feel like the COVID-19 pandemic increased our need to connect with other people. And for our young people, who generally experienced a level of isolation and disconnect coupled with the strange disconnected connect of technology and social media, they crave it more than ever, whether they ever verbalize or even realize it or not.

There are ways to bring storytelling into the classroom at any age level. Here are some suggestions:

When sharing your own experiences with students, if students are having a hard time grasping a concept or are dealing with something emotional, share a story about your past and experiences as a young student. This allows the students to feel that you understand what they're going through and perhaps find some inspiration and answers to their own problems.

A training I did a few years ago offered insight for a teacher of a sixth grader who was really struggling to write. This teacher was ranting (or *telling*—see Muscle #3) during the training that she could not get through to this kid (QTIP—see Muscle #1) who was really defiant and refused to write. After she told us all about her frustrations, I asked if she had ever tried to relate to the student's experience. She was baffled by the question at first. She had "told" him over and over how much he "needed" to learn to write because he could not have a good future if he couldn't write. The more he pulled back and resisted, the more she pushed in and told him all the reasons he *had* to learn to write.

It was a dynamic that was deteriorating fast, and there were no winners.

In my conversation with this teacher, I shared with her that what I heard was her worry for him, her care for him, and her passion for teaching. She was a bit taken back that I summarized what I was experiencing with such compassion and understanding after she had just blasted her frustration about him to the entire room.

Then I wondered with her: What might this student be feeling? I asked her, "What subject was really tough for you in school?" She told me, "Math." I asked her how she felt when it was math time in school. She told us all that she felt stupid, incapable, and pretty helpless. She shared that math caused many tears and miserable late nights over homework and anxious test prep. I asked her if she had ever considered sharing this with her student. I asked her to think about how he might be feeling every time she asks him to write and then rails at him in desperation to get him to write, even one sentence.

Jump forward to the end of the day as we were packing up from the two 2.5-hour workshops we facilitated. The teacher of said student had been in the morning session, and as I was loading my car, she hurried up to me, excited and a bit out of breath. She shared that she'd really heard our conversation, and after lunch she'd shared her math story with her student. She did two things beyond the story:

She approached him individually and asked if she could share something with him, and he agreed.

At the end of the story, she asked him if he had ever felt like she did in math but in writing—every time she asked him to write. He did.

At this point the teacher got emotional, and her voice broke as she told me, that afternoon, this student wrote more than he had the first 4 months of school. He just needed to know he was understood, not alone, and believed in.

She became a believer in storytelling and realized that to tell a personal story does not weaken us; it humanizes us.

continued

continued from previous

Introduce a new topic through a story. Telling a story is a great icebreaker and a way to introduce a concept. It allows the student to relate better to the content and gets them interested before learning. It could also allow you to activate prior knowledge, which also assists students in learning new content.

Use a story to present a concept. A story can allow students to retain information in a more creative, memorable way. It can even provoke their interest in learning a new concept. Make it relevant, make it engaging, and watch how it can open even some of your most resistant students. You can also ask them to share stories, when appropriate, for deeper engagement.

So start flexing! Like any SEL Muscle, the more you use it, the stronger and more comfortable it gets.

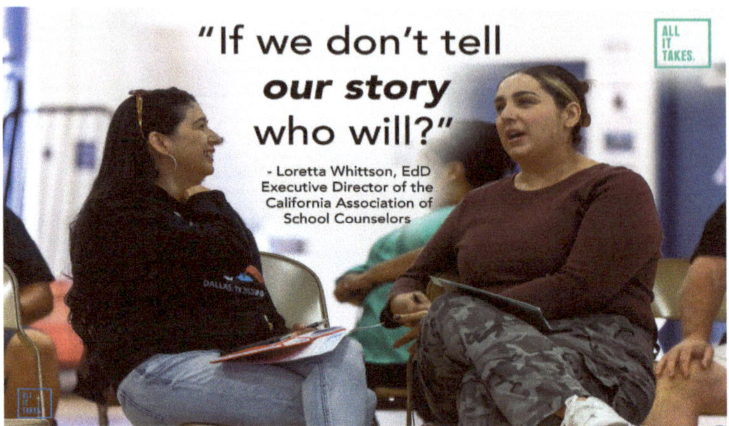

STORYTELLING FOR FAMILIES AND CARERS

Many of us had a parent, a grandparent, or some adult who looked after us who would tell us stories of how much harder it was for them when they were your age. Does this sound at all familiar?

> "When I was your age, I walked 2 miles to and from school, even in the dead of winter."

My grandpa used to tell me this all the time. He was from Canada and had to walk in the snow to school. So when I would complain that I had to walk four blocks to school in Southern California weather, he would tell me how good I had it and how bad he had it. I never even saw snow fall until I was in seventh grade, so I could not relate at all to what he was saying. I could imagine, but that is not the same as relating. Had my grandpa simply said, "I understand how you feel. I always wanted to get a ride to school, too, and I envied those kids who did." I would have related to his feelings even though our stories were 50 years and two countries apart.

> "When I was your age, children had respect for their elders."

Et cetera, et cetera, and now look! Here we are as the elders ourselves. And, of course, there is much that can be said about the vast differences between our young lives and the lives of young people today. Now does this sound recently familiar?

"When I was your age, we couldn't look things up on the internet. We had to go research at the library."

"When I was your age, we didn't have cell phones and couldn't communicate with our friends all the time."

"When I was your age, I had to go to school and help around the house and yard. I even cooked dinner for the entire family."

And so on and so on.

But would these statements, while true for us, help us to connect with the young people in our lives? Would they help them to feel heard and seen? Do they make the young person feel supported or judged?

Generation gaps have always existed. It is the way of the world to expand and change, and our young people did not ask for these dramatic shifts. **They're just living in the world and systems that we adults have created.** While acknowledging how very different many aspects of their life are from ours when we were their age, we must also see the emotional parallels connecting them.

Let's take the first statement. Would you have liked to have easily accessible research options to use for school assignments when you were young? Can you see that, even with information readily available, it doesn't necessarily make an assignment easier? In some cases students may be overwhelmed by the information, often with conflicting facts and opinions, and they may still feel unsure of how to effectively package it for an assignment. Having so much knowledge at their fingertips doesn't automatically make things easy for them.

Imagine making a shift:

"When I was young, I often struggled with research projects. I didn't even know where to start. Even when I could find all of the information that I needed, I still didn't feel confident about my writing skills. Can I do anything to help you? Is there anything specific that is tripping you up? Sometimes explaining your points first can make it easier. I want you to learn to work independently, but I'm here for support if you need it."

"They don't care how much we know until they know how much we care."

- Tom Hixon

Do you think that has more potential to connect with your young person? The objective is for you to offer support and to convey that you have faith in their abilities and also acknowledge that it can still be hard to complete the project.

Let's look at the second common statement.

"When I was your age, we didn't have cell phones and couldn't communicate with our friends all the time."

Would you have liked more connection and interaction with your friends when you were young? Can you also see that a cell phone is a potential burden? Kids feel the need to be constantly plugged in, to keep up socially, and to not miss out on anything. Sounds exhausting!

They most likely will never admit to it, but the relentless need to communicate, both on social media and with peers, can be overwhelming. When can they unplug and not experience FOMO, not be judged, and feel heard and supported?

Sadly, it doesn't seem to happen often enough, and I believe, and research shows, that their rise in anxiety and mental disorders, at increasingly younger ages, illustrates the point (Columbia University, 2025; Katella, 2024; World Health Organization, 2024). So give your child the gift of stories that share a feeling between you, stories that validate their experiences while still embracing your own.

STORYTELLING CAUTIOUS CONSIDERATIONS

Storytelling can be fun for both the speaker and the listener. It is a powerful tool when used to connect young people to the lived experience of others while allowing them to sort out the meaning for themselves. As different as people are to one another, so are stories and how people interpret their meaning. The power in storytelling lies in the listeners' personal interpretations and the speaker's curiosity about the listeners' takeaways. There are a couple key cautions to watch for as you take on using the SEL Muscle #4, Storytelling.

Caution #1: Comparisons

Storytelling can be amazing one minute and a minute later digress into a tale that starts comparing pain, and often even starts on a path of outdoing each other's problems, like there is a prize for the story or situation that is "judged" to be worse than another. Currently, in middle school, in high school, and even in workplaces, there is a growing desire for students to outdo each other's mental health challenges (Bakalos, 2023; Simonds, 2024). Students are trying to "out pain" one another, which in itself is socially and emotionally unhealthy and needs to be addressed expertly. An example from my adult life that drove this point home for me happened after my dad passed away.

I was having a conversation with a dear friend, someone who was like a mom to me as I was growing up. She was grieving after having lost one of her pets, a furry family member. As she was sharing her sadness and loss, she suddenly stopped short, gasped, and said, "I am so so sorry to be sharing this. You lost your dad, and this is only my cat." She herself did the comparison—I was not experiencing that at all. All I was feeling was compassion for her and her loss, her grief.

It occurred to me at that moment that while stories and circumstances differ, feelings associated with them are the bridge to understanding and trust. She felt bad that somehow my grief was worse than hers and she "should not" talk about hers because I had it worse. She was comparing stories, not feelings, and I could see that grief was just grief. We had a good conversation after and decided together that we both had the right to feel what we were feeling, and we could both support each other without comparing who had it "worse."

Caution #2: Remember Your Audience

It is always important to think about the stories that you share, why you are telling them, and what you intend for their messages to be. There is quite a fine line between telling young people too much information about our personal lives and what is appropriate to share. I hear this from administrators all the time, that their teachers are worried about telling vulnerable stories that will reduce their authority. The opposite is true actually: More respect is gained when one humanizes lived experience. An example of this would be the difference between the following stories:

> **"Last night was rough. I had a big fight with my partner, and my teenager came home after curfew, so I didn't get much sleep."**

In my opinion, this amount of detail would not be appropriate to share with students. This might be a better consideration:

"Good morning. How are all of you? I want to share with you that this has not been my best morning. Everything seemed hard last night and this morning I am feeling tired and stressed. Has anyone else ever had one of those mornings and came to school tired and stressed? OK, right, we are all human—thank you for understanding. I will be working to reset my day in a better direction, and I appreciate your support."

If you are working with older teens and they are interested in more detail and you are intentional about the impact you want your story to have for them, perhaps a little more detail would be helpful:

"Last night I lost it a bit. I didn't handle a challenging situation very well. I found myself yelling and then giving my family the silent treatment. This morning I am feeling badly about all that, and I need to clean it up with my family after work today. No matter what they are doing or saying, I still need to be in control of my reactions. Can anyone relate? What are the ways you manage your reactions, and how do you clean it up once you've crossed a line? Here is what I plan to do that has worked for me in the past . . ."

Storytelling Review

THE BASICS

- Storytelling is a centuries-old communication tool used to deliver messages and build connections.
- Storytelling focuses on using personal experiences and feelings to relate to others and create trust.
- Effective storytelling involves short, authentic, and relatable stories that spark emotion and convey meaningful messages.

WHY BOTHER?

- Stories are the oldest form of teaching, helping to bond communities and provide answers to life's big questions.
- Storytelling helps students feel understood and creates mutual understanding.
- Sharing personal stories can humanize educators and carers, making them more approachable and relatable.

SECRET SAUCE

- Tell stories to connect with young people, not to teach or convince.
- Keep in mind that authenticity is key—young people can detect what's real and crave genuine connections.
- Remember that effective stories don't need to be dramatic or elaborate; they simply need to create a cord of connection and relatability.

AWESOME OUTCOMES

- Help students feel less alone in their experiences and emotions, and thus foster resilience and good mental health.
- Improve information retention by making abstract concepts more interesting, concrete, and relatable.
- Create a more supportive and understanding classroom and home environment.

TIPS FOR SUCCESS

- **Model authenticity:** Educators should share personal, age-appropriate stories that relate to students' experiences and emotions, focusing on connection rather than teaching. Parents should tell stories that validate their children's feelings, even if the circumstances differ, to build understanding and trust.
- **Keep stories concise and relatable:** Educators should aim for short, easy-to-understand stories that spark emotion and maintain student interest. Parents should avoid lengthy comparisons about generational differences and instead focus on sharing relatable emotional experiences from their youth.
- **Practice mindful sharing:** Educators should carefully consider which personal stories are appropriate to share, balancing vulnerability with maintaining professional boundaries. Parents should be cautious about oversharing personal details, focusing instead on stories that offer support and acknowledge their children's challenges without judgment.

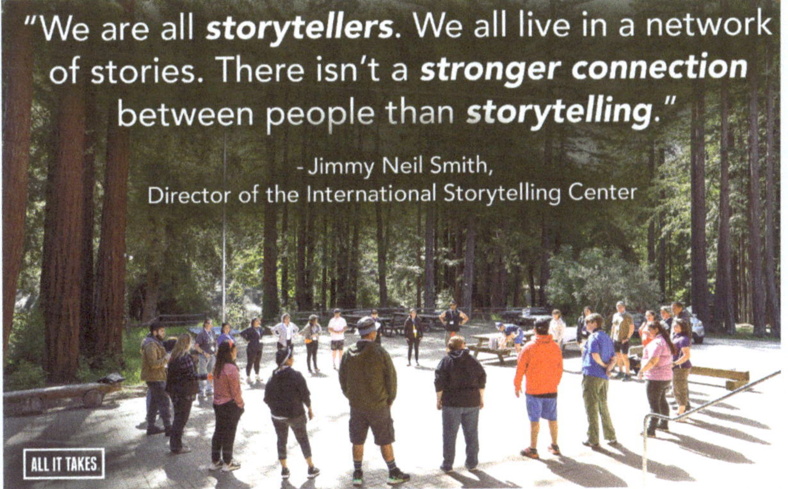

Storytelling Pause and Reflect

NOTICE.

- Think about people in your life who you appreciate hearing stories from. Think of those whose stories you never want to hear; in fact, you do everything you can to avoid them.
- What are the differences in storytelling technique and intention?
- Who do you learn from, and who makes you feel like they are wagging a finger in your face?
- What feelings come up for you, and what behaviors follow those feelings?
- Think about your storytelling. What do you hope to accomplish in telling stories? What feelings in others do you hope to evoke? What behaviors do you want to elicit? Does it work?

CHOOSE.

- If you noticed that others, or yourself, are ineffective in creating the outcomes you want, what do you want instead?
- What feelings and behaviors do you want to experience?
- What do you want to create for others?

ACT.

- Reflecting on what you want to create in relationship with others, identify what stories you are willing to tell that would help others understand you more and support them in understanding themselves more.
- Determine to whom and when you will tell your first story.
- Tell it, then reflect: What went well? Did it have your desired effect?
- Be sure to explore the obstacles that might get in the way, and have a plan to overcome them in real time.

MUSCLE #5

Curiosity

INTRODUCTION TO CURIOSITY

How long has it been since we've thought about the awe we felt as a child when something new would show up in front of us? When a bug flew past and suddenly that was the most amazing or startling thing ever? When a thunderstorm blew in and we were filled with delight or fear or some other uniquely personal experience? Remember the awe of seeing an airplane or a caterpillar, a garbage truck or the ocean?

How about when we wondered about that other child in our class or at the park—would they like to play with us? Was it easy to strike up a conversation, or did we find ourselves wanting so badly to say something but the sound and words just wouldn't come?

A curious thing happened for many of us as we matured into adulthood; the wonder we felt, the curiosity that drove our imagination and zest for learning, faded. It was replaced with "knowing," otherwise known as "judgment." It may seem counterintuitive, but bringing back wonder and curiosity instead of coming from a point of all-knowing authority is a transformative approach to use with young people. Curiosity is a great bridge-builder, but knowing can be a great divider. Let's take a look.

CURIOSITY FOR EDUCATORS

I once had a colleague who at the beginning of the year (or anytime a new student started attending her class) would ask her students to draw a map and timeline of a typical school morning. What time did they wake up? Did anyone get them up? What did they have for breakfast? Did they spend it with anyone? What did they feel like? How did they get to school? What did they encounter on the way? How did school feel when they arrived? Et cetera, et cetera. She was curious about the lives that her students were leading and knew that the more that she knew about them, the better she could be at meeting their individual needs. Of course, that is not to say that she could meet all their particular challenges or wishes, but she had a much better understanding of what they were going through. This is also a reason for parent–teacher conferences: to see who is supporting and influencing our students at home, which can inform how we interact with them at school.

As much as you are able, learn small details about your students. If you facilitate an activity like All My People, you can keep track of which students cross the circle for each prompt. Ask questions in class or when you have them in small groups or one-on-one, and keep a little journal for yourself with details about them. You don't have to make this into an arduous task; just create little notes so that you can remember things about them. It goes a long way when they see that you are interested in them as individuals and not just as one of the masses. You can also use opportunities to tell appropriate details about yourself, which can open the door to them sharing more about themselves, laying Muscle #4, Storytelling, over your curiosity for deeper connection.

ALL MY PEOPLE

Here's the simplest way to play this activity:

Circle students up, if possible (standing or sitting at desks works, too), and share that together you are going to do an activity called All My People. Everyone participates, and when it is your turn, you will think of something true for you and say to the group, "All My People who _____," and fill in the blank.

For instance, to start the activity, you might say:

- "All My People who love to walk their dog"
- "All My People who enjoy reading more than watching TV"
- "All My People who had a hard time waking up this morning"
- "All My People who sometimes feel worried about the future"
- Anything that's true for you and appropriate for the group

After a prompt is shared, everyone for whom it is also true will pass through the middle of the circle, high-five someone on their way, and end up in a completely different spot in the circle. The last person to a new spot is now the sharer. This goes on for at least five sharers and up to everyone participating.

Why does curiosity help so much? One reason is that it lives in a space of nonjudgment. If I had to choose the opposite of curiosity, I would make a case that it is judgment. We know from our own lives and experiences with others that judgment generally shuts down whomever it is directed at. It is a closed door, rather than the open one that curiosity provides. I know that curiosity doesn't always create a wide-open easily accessible door, but it can open a tiny proverbial window somewhere, an opportunity (however small) for us to wedge ourselves into in hopes of connecting with our students and each other.

Let's look at a behavior that we'd like to see modified, if not eliminated. A student fails to turn in their homework, time after time. If you skip to judgment, which is "knowing," thoughts such as these emerge:

- **"This kid is unteachable. I can't make exceptions for them."**
- **"They're lazy. They're being disrespectful by doing it time and time again."**
- **"Nothing seems to make a difference. Why should I try if they don't care?"**

The door is closed for any progress or point of access as soon as your mind determines that you know what is happening for them. You essentially form a conclusion about the student, and there is no wiggle room for the situation to change. Your students can tell when you've lost hope in them; they barely had it themselves to begin with, and now things are going downhill with no chance of a redirect. You can keep demanding that they do the assignments, to which they generally dig in harder with their lack of effort. You are left exemplifying the definition of insanity: doing the same thing over and over, yet expecting different results. This unproductive cycle often triggers us into poorly executed SEL Muscles #1 (QTIP), #2 (the Power of "I"), and #3 (Ask vs. Tell).

On the other hand, you could get curious. You could not take it personally, offer the benefit of the doubt, and then start to imagine what could be going on with your student. Maybe home is a battlefield, where homework is the last thing on their minds. Maybe they are genuinely lost in a way that you haven't identified yet, and they don't know how to begin telling you how much they don't know (consider times in your life when shame kept you quiet). Maybe they are battling depression or some other anxiety disorder and cannot focus in a way that allows them to do work on their own outside of the classroom. Maybe there is a food shortage in the home, and they are legitimately hungry and functioning poorly.

We can identify a lot of what is going on with our students—their behaviors, who they're dating, if they seem listless or have big mood shifts, and so on—but as we know, people are like icebergs. We only see a very small portion of what is going on and frequently have no real idea of what is happening beneath the surface. Also, by nature teenagers especially can be very covert creatures, hiding what they don't want others to see like it is a part-time job. Even young children have often already internalized what is OK to talk about and what is not, based on social stigmas, household secrecy policies (implicit and explicit), and paying attention to cultural norms.

A trainer who works for me tells this story from his experience as a middle school teacher:

In the lunchroom, a teacher was complaining about a disrespectful student who fell asleep every day in her class. It was very unflattering commentary. My trainer, Alex, was concerned because he didn't have the same experience in his class. He left the interaction curious about this young boy and found him at lunch break. He checked in with him, genuinely: "How are you today? I am asking because I am concerned about you. I heard that you have a hard time staying awake during first period." The student responded, appreciating that he was checked in on, and told Alex that after school each day he does his homework and then goes to work at his family's restaurant until after 1:00 a.m. He sleeps because he is exhausted.

Alex thought about this and acknowledged the student for the effort he was making to support his family and appreciated that he actually even got to school each day, on time. Then he decided to approach the boy's teacher. Here he was careful, wanting to invite the teacher to hear what he had found out without creating a situation where the teacher felt defensive. So he asked her, "I had a conversation with your student, and I found out some information about him that surprised me. Would you be open to hearing what I found out?" She was open and then very surprised by the information.

This approach worked in the end for all parties. The first-period teacher was open to understanding and then willing to work with the student to find a solution that supported him while helping her feel valued. The two of them met, they made a plan, and the rest of the year their relationship was mutually productive and caring.

Curiosity means that instead of rushing to correct or direct, we take a pause to observe and consider a child's perspective, intentions, and needs.

This inquisitive mindset not only builds trust and fosters empathy but also models the kind of exploratory thinking we want young people to develop. They learn that asking questions and seeking understanding are valuable tools for navigating the world. They learn not to judge others quickly and to try to understand the motivations of others. By staying curious, we step into the young person's world rather than trying to mold it prematurely through our own lens. This new dynamic allows us to feel less stressed because we benefit both from the emotion of giving grace and from the calm it offers our nervous systems when we don't jump to conclusions.

Curiosity can be an antidote to the frustration and impatience that can arise when kids challenge us. It transforms misunderstandings into puzzles we can solve together and allows us to approach parenting and teaching with fresh eyes—each day, each child, and each interaction holds the potential for discovery. This makes our days more interesting and far less frustrating!

Curiosity for an educator is also like having a secret key to unlocking a child's potential and a deeper relationship with them. When we stay curious, we approach each child with an openness that makes space for their unique way of seeing and understanding the world. Instead of getting frustrated or jumping to conclusions, curiosity invites us to ask, "Why is this happening? What's behind this behavior? What can I learn here?" This shift in mindset does something powerful: It builds a bridge of connection, one based on genuine interest and compassion.

When children sense that we're truly interested in understanding them—not just managing or correcting them—they feel safe to share more of themselves. They see that questions are not a form of interrogation but a way to build trust and gain insight. Curiosity transforms discipline from punishment into an opportunity to learn together, making even difficult moments feel constructive.

This curious approach also benefits us as adults. It keeps us from falling into the trap of assumptions and habits, instead refreshing our perspectives and keeping our interactions lively and meaningful. By modeling curiosity, we help children see the world as a place of endless exploration, where mistakes are opportunities to grow and understanding is always within reach.

Curiosity has profound benefits for both the adult and the child in educator–student relationships. When we engage with curiosity, our brains shift into a learning-oriented state, activating pathways that promote positive, flexible thinking. Rather than reacting automatically or emotionally when a child is challenging, curiosity lets us take a step back, reducing the likelihood of a stress-driven reaction.

Over time, a curiosity-driven approach fosters resilience, creativity, and emotional intelligence in both adults and children, setting a neurological foundation for lifelong learning and healthy relationships. In essence, curiosity isn't just a mindset; it's a brain state that enriches the social and cognitive development of everyone involved.

Another powerful benefit of curiosity is its ability to defuse defensiveness—both in ourselves and in others. When we approach a situation with curiosity, we shift from a judgmental mindset to an exploratory one, which can lower our own mental defenses and also encourage openness in our young people. This means that instead of seeing feedback or mistakes as threats, we're more likely to see them as interesting data or clues.

For example, if a child resists doing something, instead of reacting with frustration, a curious mindset might prompt us to ask, "What's behind this resistance?" or "How could we make this task feel more doable?" This approach softens the interaction and makes the student feel heard, decreasing their need to push back or defend themselves. Curiosity in this way acts almost like a neutralizer; it turns potentially tense moments into opportunities for dialogue, where both sides feel more relaxed and receptive. Over time, this dynamic builds a relationship founded on trust, making it easier to communicate and cooperate on a deeper level.

Although it has been a painfully slow needle to move, long-emerging best-practice pedagogy and abundant research are driving education ecosystems to begin embracing new teaching practices (Evans et al., 2023; Liu et al., 2024; Paulos, 2020; Stenger, 2014). These newer strategies create opportunities for young learners to use their curiosity to acquire knowledge and practical application rather than the age-old "I give you information, you memorize it and pass a test, and we all move on while forgetting most of what we memorized and never learned" philosophy.

So it is up to us to play detective whenever we can. We must get curious, stay in inquiry, and notice when judgment hijacks our curiosity. It is helpful to look beyond the behaviors even when needing to correct or redirect behavior challenges. Also with young people, often they don't understand what is going on below their own behaviors, as they generally don't know yet about neural pathways, triggers, how their amygdalas work, and so on. You may have heard of the idea that you may not remember what happened, but your nervous system does. Young people may have traumas that they don't even remember, yet like grass growing through the concrete sidewalk, their behaviors can be results of what happened to them. This short film offers a powerful insight into this concept: www.allittakes.org/atrustedspace/educatorinsights.

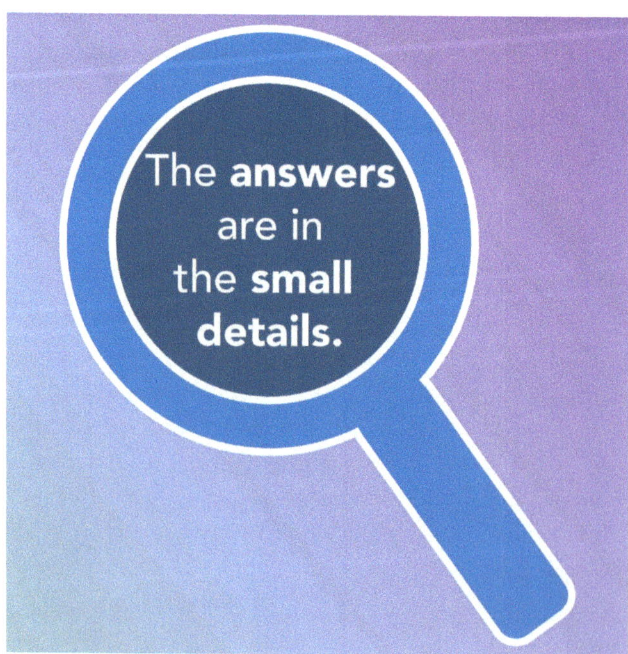

On a personal note, and with her permission, I'm sharing with you a story that happened with my sister, who for over 40 years had autoimmune health concerns that came close to taking her life. When she was a young girl and then again as a teenager, she was assaulted by people she trusted. In a protective response, her mind shut down all memory of the first assault, and she believed she had emotionally handled the second. However, her nervous system remembered and triggered what became autoimmune responses that resulted in severe anaphylactic and other allergic reactions to an ever-increasing list of foods and environmental stimuli. Her nervous system worked hard to reduce all exposures, and her life became defined as one of constant illness and retreat from things many of us take for granted, such as being in nature, traveling, and even enjoying food. Her life became small, and my gregarious, fun, and passionate sister started to shrink from almost everything. This lasted until she found support that helped her understand, and then do the work to reverse, her nervous system hijack and retrain it. The changes in my sister feel like a miracle. She now pets animals, eats dairy, hikes in nature, and travels. She did the hard work to uncover what no one understood when she was a young girl. I don't know if any of this could have been avoided or healed before her nervous system took such an uncompromising grip on her well-being, but I often wonder if a deeper dive into being curious about what was going on with her could have supported her wellness much earlier.

How Can You Truly See Your Students?

What does it truly mean to see your students? You can try an activity like Home Trees, similar to Family Trees, but more inclusive, as not every child knows or lives with their family of origin.

HOME TREES

Traditionally, teachers ask students to create Family Trees, and this is challenging for many students. For instance, an adopted child may interpret "family" as someone they have never known, which may leave them feeling excluded from the activity. This is a reality for a dear friend of mine who never felt like she could put a "right" answer on her Family Tree. A Home Tree would frame the project around "the people you live with, who care for you, who are special people in your life." This may include people outside the home but who are instrumental in caretaking and creating a sense of security. Some students may even add pets or trusted friends. The gift in this is that it creates an opportunity to celebrate all children in their personal lived experience. The outcomes of this are a great way for educators to learn more and bring more intrinsic curiosity to the classroom.

Also, it is not necessarily useful for you to understand them better by knowing who their great grandparent was, but it can be extremely helpful to know how a student is currently living. What support systems do they have, or lack, at home? As hard as it was, a small silver lining of the COVID-19 pandemic was that in some cases you could see into students' homes; see what resources they had, or did not have, available; see who was supporting them; and see how they lived in terms of calm or chaos, independence or dependence. When you know where a young person is coming from, it is easier to understand them and to put the SEL Muscles to work. It can be easier to not take it personally when a student behaves in a certain way if you can see some of the root causes for the behavior. That does not mean that you need to excuse destructive or distracting actions, but it can help you to contextualize them and not take them personally. If you see how verbal interactions are handled in students' homes and communities, it can help you with your *asks* (see Muscle #3) and with what stories you think will be relevant to them (see Muscle #4). It can create necessary points of access for you to potentially reach them more effectively.

Throughout it all, maintain genuine curiosity. What could make class more engaging for this student? What might be going on with them that they want to communicate with their friends so much? How can you reach them where they're at and create a win-win for both of you? Are they used to only receiving attention when they act out, and how can you change that dynamic in your class? Would changing their seat work? Would giving them a leadership role work? Are they having trouble understanding content and want to interrupt class to cover it up? Is something happening in their work or social life that is making them behave disruptively? Are they hungry, or is it a time of day when it is particularly hard for them to focus? There are so many things to wonder about our students, to try to imagine and determine what is going on below their surface behaviors.

CURIOSITY SAVED ME AS AN EDUCATOR

It kept me from burning out and made my work far more enjoyable. As a new counselor, when I had not yet developed the Curiosity Muscle well, I often thought to myself, "Ugh, and I'm the one in charge of changing this student's behavior."

continued

continued from previous

I felt ill equipped to handle the shifts needed. I began embracing curiosity, truly wanting to look at the root of every problem and not the red flags flying in their metaphorical branches, screaming for attention, often in the most exasperating ways possible. When I could move beyond their surfaces—the angry, sad, or checked-out tips of their individual icebergs—it changed the whole game. I felt more successful than I ever had before, and my relationships with students helped to reinforce those feelings. Regularly flexing Muscle #5, Curiosity, can make what may have become an often-frustrating classroom dynamic into a place of shared experiences, trust, and even some much-needed levity.

CURIOSITY FOR FAMILIES AND CARERS

To me, there is no better superpower to develop as a parent or carer than the power to stay calm and be slow to react, using pauses to craft intentional and constructive responses. I know what you might be thinking: "Lori, it would be easier to learn to fly!" I recognize how challenging it is, when our kids can wear our every last nerve, and we feel unsupported, unappreciated, and taken for granted. But it can be done, and through its development, you can maintain your sanity and develop better relationships with your children.

Is it easy to stay curious when they're coming at you with the wide range of misdirected emotions that they seem to so easily hurl at us?

Definitely not.

Is it worth it? I believe that it is. As a current mother of adult children, I recognize that their experience of their childhood in many ways differs from mine, and I must work hard to not feel blamed, victimized, or quite frankly even too bothered by what they perceived. I try to stay curious and acknowledge why they feel the ways they do and stay curious with myself about how I will choose to process and use the information.

Being curious is one of the most valuable approaches we can take as parents. When we allow ourselves to approach situations with genuine curiosity, we open the door to understanding, growth, and a deeper connection with our children. It's easy to think that, as adults, we know best; but when we set aside that assumption and ask questions instead, we're not only giving our children space to express themselves—we're also showing them that their thoughts and feelings matter. Curiosity becomes a bridge between us and our children, creating a safe and open environment where they feel heard and respected.

In moments of conflict or frustration, curiosity is an incredible tool for maintaining peace. Rather than reacting with impatience or judgment, we can pause and ask ourselves, "Why might they be acting this way? What could they need right now?" These questions shift our focus to understanding rather than control. It's like rewiring our responses, helping us see beyond the immediate behavior to what's going on underneath. This shift doesn't just help resolve issues with less conflict; it strengthens the trust between us and our children because they know we're willing to look deeper and be there with empathy, not judgment.

Curiosity also fosters a sense of discovery in our relationship with our kids. When we approach caring for them as an ongoing learning journey, we become more flexible and open-minded. Each stage of their lives brings new perspectives and changes, and curiosity helps us adapt to those changes rather than resisting them. Instead of expecting young people to stay within the lines of our expectations, we can step into their world, discovering who they are at each stage, what they love, and what challenges them. This builds a foundation of mutual respect and understanding, setting a tone of acceptance that encourages them to be themselves.

One unusual benefit of curiosity is that it reduces the experience of time pressure, which can be especially powerful when dealing with kids. When we're curious, we tend to get into a flow state—some call it being "in the zone"—where we feel more absorbed in the present moment. This heightened focus can make us feel less hurried, allowing us to experience interactions and situations with a sense of openness and even wonder. In the dynamics of a busy modern household, this can be a true game-changer.

In this state, we're more receptive and less critical, which in turn can improve our patience and enjoyment in the moment. Instead of viewing challenging situations with kids as obstacles we need to quickly "fix" or move past, curiosity helps us experience them with a sense of discovery, perhaps even wonder. This unusual benefit creates a more relaxed dynamic, where the whole family feels less rushed and more engaged, which can turn everyday challenges into meaningful shared experiences. If we are able to add humor to the mix, even better.

When we choose to stay curious about our kids' choices and motivations, we become a source of safety and support in their lives.

They are likely to feel that they can bring their true selves to us—without fear of harsh reactions or disapproval. Curiosity tells them that we're on their side, willing to listen and understand, rather than labeling them or jumping to conclusions. As a result, they're more likely to share their thoughts, feelings, and experiences with us, knowing we'll respond with empathy and openness rather than judgment or punishment.

By fostering this trust, we give them space to explore who they are and learn from their decisions. They see us not as critics but as partners in their journey, someone they can turn to even when they're unsure or when they've made mistakes. Curiosity helps them understand that mistakes aren't something to hide from us; instead, they're opportunities for learning, supported by someone who cares deeply and without conditions. Over time, this builds a foundation of respect and reliability in our relationship.

Our kids will likely also develop stronger self-confidence and problem-solving skills because, rather than fearing our judgment, they feel encouraged to reflect on their actions. They learn to think through choices more critically because we've modeled thoughtful, nonreactive behavior. Rather than being motivated by fear of punishment, they're guided by an understanding of their own values, knowing we've taken the time to understand what's meaningful to them. When they feel seen and understood, they're more inclined to see themselves with the same compassion we extend to them, building healthier self-perception.

Of course, you already know many details about your children, but they are always changing and expanding. As much as they will let you, try to stay up with their likes, their dislikes, their friends, their struggles, and so on. As a parent myself, I know that they can become covert at certain ages and resistant to letting you into their burgeoning worlds. Despite the fact that they may live with you and/or have grown up with you, they generally still spend a fair amount of time away from home. If they attend school, that is for hours every day, and often the older they get, the more they will spend time with friends and join extracurriculars. The question "How was your day?" is often met with "Good" or "Fine" and doesn't necessarily give the information that you'd like to know to stay aware of what is happening with them.

So how else can you gain access into their worlds? What strategies can you use to sneak into their minds and see what is going on in there? It is a delicate balance to maintain not wanting to be too intrusive and giving them their independence, especially as they get older, while also wanting to stay informed of what is developing for them in their social circles, interests, and so on.

When they don't want to share, it can be helpful to respect their boundaries and to not take it personally. It is part of the process of growing up for children to want to separate from their families and carers and assert their independence, but it can still feel hard when they go from children who see you as their central figures to young people who want to develop their identities with minimal input from you. As much as possible, let them know that you're interested but also respect what they do and don't want to share. If they begin exhibiting different behaviors, especially ones that challenge you, stay in curiosity as much as possible. It can be extremely helpful to keep your proverbial communication door wide open, letting them know that you want to support their changes and development and will only interfere without being asked if the situation truly warrants it. Try to stay aware of who they are spending time with and how they are learning to build their own boundaries and identity, without judgment. Ideally, they will feel comfortable coming to you when they do need advice or support, and you want them to know that you are a safe space for them to express themselves and what they want and need.

AGAIN, USE CURIOSITY!

"I wonder why they are acting like that"

goes a lot further than

"I can't believe they are acting like that."

Like the observant sponges they are, children can tell when you are asking out of genuine curiosity and interest and when you are judging their choices. Although their world is different from the one when you grew up, try to remember how you wanted adults to treat you when you were their age.

Genuine curiosity can go a long way in maintaining the relationship of trust and openness that will serve you both well.

This SEL Muscle requires frequent flexing. When our 6-year-old draws on our beautiful walls, when our teenager sneaks out past curfew, when our middle schooler suddenly doesn't want to go to a class they loved previously, even when our children tell us they wish they had been born to another family (always a gut punch)—how can we maintain our equilibrium and look for the reasons behind the actions? When we stay curious, we create an atmosphere where they're more likely to let us into their worlds. And that's one where we can avoid greater frustration! They're more inclined to view us as trusted confidants, knowing we'll approach them with kindness, acceptance, and a true desire to understand them. With that, we have a solid foundation for all of the boat-rocking that is sure to happen while raising young people.

CURIOSITY CAUTIOUS CONSIDERATIONS

For both families and educators, the line is a fine one between being curious and being what young people would see as nosy or invasive. Once you find out some things, there may be a desire to discover more, but it is important to still let them have their own boundaries for privacy. As difficult as it can be at times, allow for curiosity to be used solely as a tool to create trust and connection. Be conscious that young people can be fiercely protective of their changing minds, bodies, relationships, thoughts, and so on, and the goal is to foster spaces of openness, not intrusiveness or judgment, while still standing firmly in the role of protector.

Caution #1: Discernment

Sometimes, for the adults in the room, it can be challenging to discern the gray area between our children's wants and needs as we navigate challenging pushback when they feel we are encroaching into their space. The following are a few areas that can be tricky:

- **Safety:** What do you need to know to be the adult responsible for keeping a child safe? Sometimes this means encroaching on highly protected adolescent privacy. For instance, checking your kids' phones, having their passwords, understanding where they surf the web, knowing where and who they hang out with, and so on are parental and educational obligations for the safety of minors. They should be non-negotiable.
- **Connection:** What do you want to know to be able to connect with your child more deeply and understand how they are developing? Are you open to knowing the reality of what your child might be thinking? Experiencing? Coping with? Adults often, on autopilot, say, "Of course I want to know"; however, the reality from the perspective of our young people can be that we are only comfortable knowing things that fit our narrative of what they "should" be going through, not necessarily *are* going through. This discernment of ourselves can help us be more openly curious and invite more trust from those we serve.
- **Nosiness:** What can you recognize as information that is beyond what you need to know and can undermine their growing independence? Adults often complain that the young people in their lives won't talk to them, even shutting down to the simple question, "How was your day?" Be sure your curiosity feels like an open invitation and not an inquisition. Remember, just because you think it is an open invitation, young people will not if they think you are prying or attached to them answering you. Remember to flex Muscle #1, QTIP, when asking them questions, it will keep you from feeling frustrated when they don't respond!

Caution #2: Allow for Autonomy

When deciding to ask questions or increase basic communication with your young people, consider these approaches to foster engagement while allowing autonomy:

- Be sure to model how to share vulnerably, and give them ample space to join you, or not, without attachment. Think Muscle #4, Storytelling. We need to be willing to share as we request of them. Our young people, in their appropriate move toward independence and adulthood, need to hear us share as much as ask. When we do not practice this, we may come across as nosy and invasive rather than genuinely curious, open, and respectful.
- As in the example in Caution #1, remember that young people will often resist answering basic questions, such as "How was your day?" Try asking specific, low-stakes questions, like these, instead:
  - "What was for lunch today?" followed by "Was it any good?"
  - "If you could change one thing about school right now, what would you change?"

Caution #3: Devices and Distractions

There is no doubt that devices are a distraction in today's world, and not only for our young people. We adults are also too often distracted by them, and it has compromised our relationship skills and mental health as well (Small et al., 2020; Tiret, 2025).

- Be willing to set aside no-devices time, and then sit through silence for as long as it takes for conversation to begin. It always does, but how long the silence needs to be depends on the dynamic of the relationship. This can be challenging at first, but the rewards far exceed the difficulty. My flagship program that I have run for over 28 years, Legacy Leadership Summit, for example, requires that students leave their phones behind for 4 days and 3 nights, and while at first it feels completely impossible for kids, the experience is life-changing. Here are some approaches you can take:

- Prohibit use of devices in car rides under 60 minutes. Instead, take turns choosing music and allow for "no music" to be a choice. You will need to accept their music, just as they'll have to accept yours. Interestingly, music choice is in itself a way to be curious about one another and things that influence you.

- Forbid use of devices during a meal or for a specific half hour (or more ideally) each evening. Make sure you are together during this time—again, even if it is silent and feels awkward at first, there is no potential for deeper connection without taking this step.

• Be creative and vigilant. Only you know the dynamics of your life and what might be available.

Curiosity Review

THE BASICS

- Curiosity is a powerful tool for educators and carers.
- Curiosity involves approaching situations with genuine interest and an open mind.
- Curiosity allows lived experiences to elevate and inform others, creating unity.

WHY BOTHER?

- Cultivating curiosity builds trust and fosters empathy.
- It transforms challenging moments into opportunities for learning and connection.
- It reduces stress and frustration and increases genuine interest in another person's interest.

SECRET SAUCE

- Shift from a judgmental mindset to an exploratory one.
- Create a safe space for open communication and self-expression.
- Bridge gaps in understanding and build stronger connections.

AWESOME OUTCOMES

- Improve relationships and foster deeper connections with young people.
- Have a more enjoyable and fulfilling experience in parenting or teaching roles.
- Help young people to feel more seen, understood, and supported.

TIPS FOR SUCCESS

- **Create intentional time:** Encourage meaningful conversations and use specific, low-stakes questions to initiate engagement. Educators, this approach fosters an environment where students feel comfortable sharing their thoughts and experiences. Parents and carers will benefit from establishing regular device-free periods at home (adults adhere to this, too), allowing for natural conversations to develop, even if it means sitting through initial silence. These moments of undistracted interaction can lead to deeper connections and understanding between adults and young people.

- **Stay genuinely interested:** Wanting to know about the reality of our young people's lives is crucial for both educators and parents/carers. Educators can demonstrate this by keeping a journal with small details about each student, to stay aware of their individual experiences and perspectives. Parents and carers should strive to stay up-to-date with their children's likes, dislikes, friends, and struggles, while being mindful of respecting boundaries and not being overly intrusive. This genuine interest helps build trust and encourages young people to open up more freely.
- **Practice patience and noninvasive inquiry:** This is essential when dealing with challenging behaviors. Educators should approach difficult student behaviors with curiosity rather than judgment, using pauses to craft intentional and constructive responses. This approach can help uncover underlying issues and lead to more effective solutions. Similarly, parents and carers can develop the ability to stay calm and be slow to react, using curiosity to understand the root causes of their children's actions and emotions. By modeling this patient and inquisitive approach, adults can create a more supportive and understanding environment for young people to grow and learn.

Curiosity Pause and Reflect

NOTICE.

- In what areas of your life do you default to snap judgments and lose the opportunity to learn that curiosity provides?
- When you react to something that a young person does, assuming things about them in the process, how does that make you feel? How do you think others you influence feel when it happens?
- What behaviors do you engage in when you assume you know why a student is behaving in a particular way? In what ways do students behave when they feel judged or misunderstood?

CHOOSE.

- If you notice areas where you forgo curiosity and leap into judgment, what would you choose to be different?
- If you created this shift, what feelings and behaviors would you experience for yourself and from others?
- What relationships do you hope to improve by being curious, and why?

ACT.

- Reflecting on what you want to create through practicing curiosity, what are three to five actionable steps to help you achieve this? Be specific.
- What hurdles might get in your way? How will you overcome them?

MUSCLE #6

Walk the Talk

INTRODUCTION TO WALK THE TALK

On the surface, the final SEL Muscle, Walk the Talk, seems obvious and easy. We hear it all the time. There's nothing uncertain in the phrase; however, in real-time action it can be challenging, and we may not be as good at it as we think. Walking the Talk means doing and saying what we teach and expect from others. It also means doing and saying what we expect from ourselves and from the world we want to live in.

Walk the Talk is an important form of integrity. It helps us make sure our hearts, minds, and actions are congruent with our values, our beliefs, and what we want our young people to exhibit. Only in this congruence can we earn the respect of others and build trusted relationships.

Our young people, especially as they become teenagers, have built-in **"hypocrisy radar,"** and they are not afraid to let us know when their alert is blasting. They can feel inconsistencies, inauthenticities, and misaligned attitudes. They know when what we are asking or relying on them to do is not aligned with what we are doing. When this happens, trust is splintered, we lose credibility, and our hard-earned authority walks right out the door.

WALK THE TALK FOR EDUCATORS

In education today, it is increasingly challenging to engage students in their own learning. They are struggling more and more to see the value of what they are learning as an asset in their own future. In fact increasingly some students can't even identify an image of a positive future for themselves. Students need to understand the value of what we are asking them to do and learn, and they need us to demonstrate it all through our words, attitudes, and actions.

Sometimes educators get into an internal power struggle, thinking, "You are the student, and I am the teacher/adult in the room. You do what I say, and *then* I might consider starting to be nicer to you or bringing a bit of humor into the classroom." In some cases, an old belief system has teachers feeling they need to be tough and unrelenting the first couple months of school so they earn the respect of students and they are not seen as weak or soft. Perhaps 50+ years ago this model worked, because students were afraid of teachers and administrators. Today, however, our young people just call this hypocrisy, and we have no way forward with them because we have no credibility. We are asking students to be cooperative, polite, flexible rule followers; however, we might come across as rude, demanding, unfriendly, and uncaring.

News flash: Everything we do and say—they're astutely watching and listening. Of course, this is old news to you, as you regularly walk into the fishbowl that your classroom can be and stand on display. And they are not just hearing and seeing. They are observing our attitude, our approach, and our expectations; they are watching whether we're authentically inclusive, when we fail, how we rebound and regroup, and our facial expressions; they are listening to our tone of voice, our under-the-breath comments, and even our deep throaty "ughs"—everything! This can be both daunting and promising, depending on the way that you look at it. It may feel like a lot of pressure, but you serve as a real role model for them. How aware are you of what you role model in all moments?

Strengthening Muscle #6, Walk the Talk, will earn you trust and respect.

From here everything is possible, including class management, high-level learning, and, by the way, fun with learning and each other!

A Note for Education Leaders

You are asking your staff to be role models for the young people they serve. They need you to do that for them. Hard stop.

Walking the Talk—translating beliefs into behaviors—is the very essence of character and integrity for both individuals and organizations. Remember:

People hear what we say, but they see what we do . . . and seeing is believing.

We judge ourselves by our intentions, but others judge us by our actions.

Words, like intentions, are only as good as the actions behind them.

You have to flex Muscle #6, Walk the Talk, to stay credible with those you serve. They have to flex the Walk the Talk Muscle to stay credible with those they serve. The trickle-down-and-back-up-again effect is real, and all of us, including our young people, need to be a part of this flow. Reciprocity builds mutual respect.

WALK THE TALK FOR FAMILIES AND CARERS

Talk about watching our every move! As the saying goes, children don't necessarily listen to what we say, but they surely watch what we do. This is even more pronounced in the home than in educational settings because your young people are able to see you at your "worst"—when you've just woken up, when you're personally stressed, when they intentionally push your buttons in ways that they typically don't with others, all the things!

Developmentally, it is appropriate for them to push against us, to see how far they can get, and to bend the boundaries that we set up with them. While we can logically know that this is what they are "supposed" to be doing, it can still feel incredibly taxing in everyday practice. They watch to see if our words align with our actions and if they consider us to be hypocrites in any sense of the word. And when they do find a chink in the armor, they may well take a pickaxe to the spot and do their best to whittle even more of our defenses away.

I find that as a parent/carer it is even more important to give ourselves grace and the ability to step away when things become too heated. We need to be vigilant about our own self-care, to be as solid as possible to stay ready for the intense scrutiny that living with young people can elicit.

As we know almost too well, they are highly observant and can quickly discern inconsistencies between what we say and do. In fact, they are looking for them! When we are able to consistently model the behaviors and values we preach, it builds trust and credibility. This trust is essential for a healthy and transparent relationship and helps young people feel secure and supported.

Imagine telling your kids that swearing is disrespectful yet you swear at the car that cut you off or when you drop a glass, etc. Besides the fact that they will view you as hypocritical, it gives them the idea that **the truth is relative**, which is a tenuous perspective for a growing mind.

Consistency in actions and words teaches children the importance of reliability and dependability. When parents and carers walk the talk, children understand that commitments and promises are to be taken seriously. This lesson helps them develop into individuals who value consistency and follow through on their own commitments.

DISCIPLINE AND BOUNDARIES

Walking the Talk is particularly important when it comes to discipline and setting boundaries. If parents enforce rules and consequences fairly and consistently, children learn the importance of discipline and self-control. However, if parents do not adhere to the rules they set, it can lead to confusion and undermine their authority.

Does this seem hard, sometimes even incredibly daunting? It definitely can be! This is also why it is important to let young people know that adults are fallible too. If (and I should say *when*) you "slip up," acknowledge it. Our young people need to know that it is OK to make mistakes and to get up and recommit to our values. When children see their adults facing challenges and persevering, they learn the value of resilience and hard work. Parents who model positive coping strategies and the ability to bounce back from lapses in judgment and behavior teach young people how to do the same, how to handle adversity and build character.

No one is asking you to be "perfect." This is also an important lesson to model for our young people. We are going to make mistakes and ask for grace, and we want to show them to do the same. As hard as it may be sometimes, it will always go a long way by admitting where we have had a misstep in our values, rather than sweeping it under the rug or telling them something like, "Well, I'm an adult, so the rules are different!" The more that we are able to have our words, actions, and beliefs clearly aligned, the better it will serve both our relationships with our young people and their positive development. This includes the admission of occasional deviations from our value systems.

Like I say with all things parenting and caring related:

Is it easy? Not always!

But is it worth it? Definitely.

WALK THE TALK CAUTIOUS CONSIDERATIONS

SEL Muscle #6, Walk the Talk, is the ultimate tool for influencing our young people. It acts as a trust- and credibility-builder and uplifts confidence and self-esteem. It feels good to model what we expect of others. Still, there are a couple of cautions to consider as you look beyond what is easy to see and deeper into your actual words, attitudes, and actions.

Caution #1: Realistic and Credible

Not all things are equal. It is important to be confident in the choices you make and the reasons you make them while still modeling what you are asking of your young folks. Without this confidence, those around you will identify and potentially leverage what they see as weakness.

For instance, it would be credible for a physical education teacher to be active during classes, demonstrating proper movements, running a few laps, and so on. It would not be reasonable, however, for a PE teacher to do that every hour for 5 straight hours, 5 days a week. What might be a good Walk the Talk example would be to use other SEL Muscles to share what you are doing with your students. "Today I did laps with period 1, so this period I am going to do warm-ups with you, next period I plan to participate in the game," and so on. Students are human, and they will be understanding when effort and information are congruent but not necessarily on full display.

An example at home might be with parents who choose to have a cocktail or glass of wine but tell their children they can't drink alcohol. Teenagers can be brutal in this confrontation. Parents should not try to justify or feel guilty about this action. If it matches your values and you feel good about it, you can talk (see SEL Muscle #4, Storytelling) about feeling so excited when you were finally legally allowed to drink and how waiting tried your patience. You can also be educated about why the law exists and stand by it in words and actions with your children. While the rules are not the same for everyone, the important thing is that you follow the rules that are yours to follow so you responsibly demonstrate this value to your children.

Caution #2: Role Clarity

Our young people need us to be the adults in their lives, not to be their friends. The boundaries between adults and young people need to be clear and reliable so everyone knows their role and their expectations. Adults need to remember that they are stewarding our young people to be healthy, independent, and thriving adults. Friendships do not have this role, and being clear on roles is critical.

One example involves what an adult tells a young person. For educators, it is appropriate for a teacher to talk about having a hard morning, a rough year, and so on. It might not be as appropriate for an educator to share the most intimate details of their domestic challenges. Friends share intimate details, often with no boundaries. Friendships are often trusted spaces where no topic is off limits. In classrooms it is important to remember that we are models for our young, not friends of them. This can be blurred at times as young people want to hear all the "stuff," and they seem to understand and offer a sympathetic ear. It is the adult who needs to walk the talk of appropriate boundaries while also being authentic. As an educator for over 30 years, I have seen both sides: too little sharing, too much sharing—it's all a matter of conscious discernment.

For families, how and what we share is deeply personal and based on individual family values. What is important to recognize is that our children need us to model and parent, to be the stronger ones in the room (even when we have to share that we are not feeling strong) and not request or require that our children be our shoulder to cry on. We need to be considerate of their age and developmental level; even if their level of language is mature, their brain is not. It is not our children's role to make our lives easier to navigate or more meaningful. We need to demonstrate personal value and care outside of our parental/guardian role.

In Walk the Talk, *all* adults can support or hinder our young people's social-emotional development. Those of us closest to them, of course, have the greatest impact, but even from a distance, the way adults act influences the way our young people act. Here are a few considerations for every adult to consider as they step out into the world each day:

- People follow actions much more than they do words.
- You are a role model. Hard stop. This means that if you want our young people to act in certain ways, then you need to lead by example and be willing to own the outcomes of your influence.
- If you want young people to be mindful of their tone and its effects on others, then you must maintain a mindful tone too.

- If you want young people to be independent, solution-focused problem-solvers, then you also need to demonstrate solution-focused problem-solving.
- If you want young people to extend the benefit of the doubt to others, then you must do the same.
- If you display a gap between what you say and what you do, you diminish the message that you are trying to send and, in many cases with young people, damage your credibility.
- Trust is harder to repair than it is to lose, so **walk with integrity**.

Walking the Talk is not just doing what we ask of others; it is doing what our role is well and with integrity, even if they don't like it or appreciate it.

Walk the Talk Review

THE BASICS

- Walking the Talk is the same thing as integrity.
- It demonstrates the behaviors you expect from others.
- It reminds you of your role as an adult steward, not a friend.

WHY BOTHER?

- Walking the Talk builds trust and credibility.
- It maintains your integrity and reinforces your messages.
- It models traits that will serve young people long into their adult years.

SECRET SAUCE

- Keep your words, actions, and values aligned to ensure credible role modeling.
- Acknowledge your mistakes and clean them up responsibly.
- Maintain appropriate boundaries while being authentic and vulnerable.

AWESOME OUTCOMES

- Improve relationships by engaging in productive communication.
- Enhance the ability to engage students in their own learning.
- Develop young people who value their worth and follow through on commitments.

TIPS FOR SUCCESS

- **Model consistency:** Educators should consistently demonstrate the behaviors and values they expect from students, such as being cooperative, polite, and flexible. Parents should align their actions with the rules and values they set for their children, avoiding hypocrisy.
- **Acknowledge mistakes:** Educators should openly admit when they make mistakes or fail to meet their own standards, showing students that adults are fallible too. Parents should acknowledge their missteps to their children rather than sweeping them under the rug, teaching them how to handle adversity, recover from setbacks, and reengage.

- **Practice self-care:** Educators should prioritize their own well-being to maintain the energy and patience needed to be effective role models. Parents should engage in regular self-care activities to stay emotionally balanced, demonstrating the importance of personal health and stress management to their children.

Walk the Talk Pause and Reflect

NOTICE.

- In what areas of your life do you ask others to do things you don't or won't do or behave in ways you excuse yourself from?
- When looking at this, how do you feel? How do you think others you influence feel?
- What behaviors do you engage in when being called out or challenged for not Walking the Talk? What behaviors do others engage in when they don't respect you?

CHOOSE.

- If you noticed areas where you do not walk the talk and the consequences of this, what would you choose to be different?
- What feelings and behaviors would you like to experience for yourself and from others?
- What relationships do you hope to improve, and why?

ACT.

- Reflecting on what you want to create through Walking the Talk, what are three to five actionable steps to help you achieve this? Be specific.
- What hurdles might get in your way? How will you overcome them?

You can't spell
SUCCESSFUL
without
SEL
ALL
IT
TAKES.

Conclusion

SEL Muscle Summary

Exploring your SEL Muscles has been a journey, one that I imagine was at times confrontational and at times a huge relief as you embraced the truth that you are enough and that evolving takes practice, patience, and committed work. Your strength in each moment depends on your well-being, which influences your ability to flex with ease and purpose. Here again are the six SEL Muscles, as a reminder of the tools you now have to create the life you wish for and deserve, all while supporting young people and those in your circle to do the same.

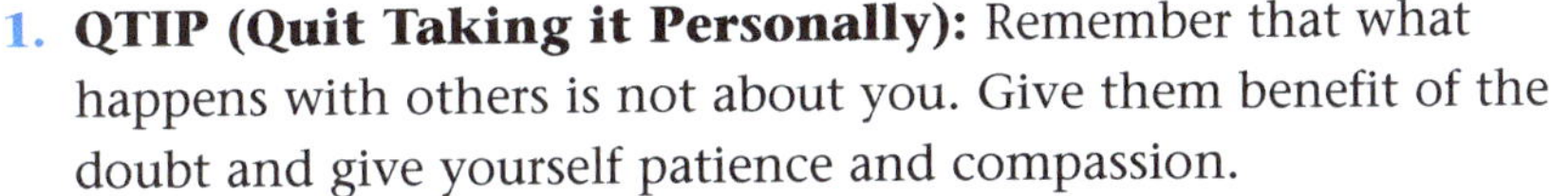

1. **QTIP (Quit Taking it Personally):** Remember that what happens with others is not about you. Give them benefit of the doubt and give yourself patience and compassion.

2. **The Power of "I":** "I" statements will give you peace and power, and others grace, as you approach conversations—especially challenging ones.

3. **Ask vs. Tell:** Your needs matter, and voicing them will help you, and others, meet them, offering more rewarding relationships and a more enjoyable life.

4. **Storytelling:** Stories shared to relate to others, and to be related to, build trusted relationships that result in deeper learning and optimistic futures.

5. **Curiosity:** Genuine curiosity about others, rather than nosiness, builds bridges and deepens interconnectedness, offering healthy relationships and productive problem-solving.

6. **Walk the Talk:** Being attentive to our actions, words, and attitudes as they relate to how we want others to do the same develops credibility and respect, offering joyful and rewarding relationships.

FINDING SUCCESS

You have taken on the two most important jobs on the planet, raising and educating our young people. In choosing to be a steward for their greatness, you wear a superhero cape while receiving no blockbuster film credit or paycheck for your dedication. You have superpowers, and you face personal kryptonite that seeks to knock you off your game. Yet you rise, every day, looking to make a difference even in the face of adversity.

Those of you reading this far, I share both roles—parent/carer and educator—with you. I have been through the trenches, and I have come out a better person with a much brighter heart and, yes, a few more gray hairs. I want you to know you are seen and you are not alone. The road is both glorious and challenging, and it does not need to be navigated alone and without tools. The SEL Muscles you have just explored are your friends: They will build you up, and they will keep you strong. They will help you recover when flexing goes badly or is missing altogether. They will help you keep loving yourself as much as you love those you care for. It took me a long time to recognize this for myself, and my hope is you get there much sooner than I did.

Growing your SEL Muscles will take much building, practice, and regular flexing. I invite you to consider the following tips for finding success with your SEL Muscles both with the young people in your life and far beyond.

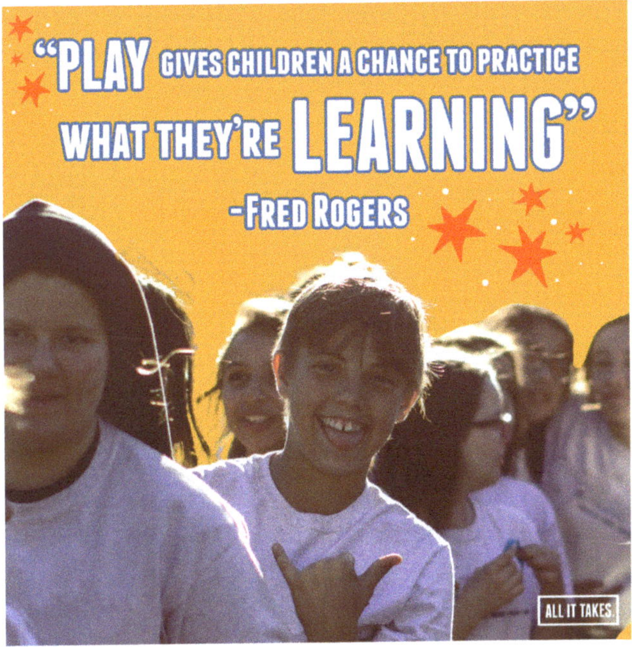

INVITE OTHERS IN!

Going it alone is a lonely trek. Find a group of trusted friends, colleagues, a parent group, or even your bestie. Use this book to learn and practice the SEL Muscles together and be each other's champions and gentle reminders. Create an accountability plan that you can hold one another to, offering support and encouragement while staying purposeful in achieving desired results. Be soft landing places and gentle nudges for one another, remembering that both of you have days when you have very little strength and flexing is near impossible.

NOTICE CHOOSE ACT YOUR WAY

The Notice Choose Act framework works for finding solutions for any challenge including redirecting behaviors. Idea: Have family meetings or classroom huddles to identify and then solve challenges that the collective is experiencing. Model the process and allow everyone to contribute to the conversation and action plans. Have everyone pick at least one small action they will commit to so the identified problem has a collective solution.

BUILD STRONG SCHOOL–HOME RELATIONSHIPS

Our students are best supported when schools embrace families and families embrace schools. Take a less traveled road, let go of past experiences and grudges, and lean into the urgency and power of this critical collaboration. Remember that while you may disagree on how to get to a solution, you all start with the same goal: to see your children and youth succeed, for them to become healthy, happy, contributing adults who care about themselves, others, and their communities. When you approach upsets with that understanding, you can use your SEL Muscles to develop or mend relationships in service to those who count on you every day. One way to do this would be to work on mastering your SEL Muscles by hosting a book study club with educators and carers—or even a book study between certificated and classified personnel. Ultimately, when you uplevel relationships in service to your young people, everyone wins, personally and collectively.

STAY THE COURSE

Even if you have to correct the course, remember your purpose and keep going. Just like we often tell our kids, practice makes perfect. Mastering the SEL Muscles may take a lifetime, but getting results that elevate your well-being and joy may only take one try. Like going to the gym to develop our physical muscles, it doesn't happen overnight, and it doesn't happen without some amount of pain. Many times it is good pain, the kind that feels productive and healthy. Commit to the journey more than the destination, and you will be on your way to more satisfying relationships with your young people, more belief in the positive impact you're having, and the peace of mind that may have felt elusive for too long.

Flex your SEL Muscles, my friends.
I will be flexing along with you!

References

Bakalos, E. (2023, March 6). *Stop making mental illness a competition.* University Girl. https://universitygirlsu.com/feelgood/2023/3/1/stop-making-mental-illness-a-competition

Columbia University. (2025). *Smartphones, social media, and their impact on mental health.* Department of Psychiatry. https://www.columbiapsychiatry.org/research/research-areas/child-and-adolescent-psychiatry/sultan-lab-mental-health-informatics/research-areas/smartphones-social-media-and-their-impact-mental-health

Evans, N. S., Burke, R., Vitiello, V., Zumbrunn, S., & Jirout, J. J. (2023, September). Curiosity in classrooms: An examination of curiosity promotion and suppression in preschool math and science classrooms. *Thinking Skills and Creativity, 49,* Article 101333. https://doi.org/10.1016/j.tsc.2023.101333

Gordon, T. (n.d.). *Origins of the Gordon Model.* Gordon Training International. https://www.gordontraining.com/thomas-gordon/origins-of-the-gordon-model/

Katella, K. (2024, June 17). *How social media affects your teen's mental health: A parent's guide.* Yale Medicine. https://www.yalemedicine.org/news/social-media-teen-mental-health-a-parents-guide

Liu, J., Tahri, D., & Qiang, F. (2024, June 5). How does active learning pedagogy shape learner curiosity? A multi-site mediator study of learner engagement among 45,972 children. *Journal of Intelligence, 12*(6), 59. https://doi.org/10.3390/jintelligence12060059

Paulos, C. (2020, January). Professional identity of adult educators in recognition of prior learning. In B. Merrill, C. C. Vieira, A. Galimberti, & A. Nizinska (Eds.), *Adult education as a resource for resistance and transformation: Voices, learning experiences, identities of student and adult educators* (pp. 299–306). Faculty of Psychology and Education Sciences, University of Coimbra, Portugal; Centre for the Research on Adult Education and Community Intervention, University of Algarve, Portugal; European Society for Research on the Education of Adults. https://esrea.org/wp-content/uploads/2021/08/ESREA-Book-2020-Complete-Filecover.pdf

Rogers, S. L., Howieson, J., & Neame, C. (2018, May 18). I understand you feel that way, but I feel this way: The benefits of I-language and communicating perspective during conflict. *PeerJ, 6,* Article e4831. https://doi.org/10.7717/peerj.4831

Simonds, G. R. (2024, November 6). Quit the suffering contest. *Psychology Today.* https://www.psychologytoday.com/us/blog/rich-encounters/202411/quit-the-suffering-contest

Small, G. W., Lee, J., Kaufman, A., Jalil, J., Siddarth, P., Gaddipati, H., Moody, T. D., & Bookheimer, S. Y. (2020, June). Brain health consequences of digital technology use. *Dialogues in Clinical Neuroscience, 22*(2), 179–187. https://doi.org/10.31887/DCNS.2020.22.2/gsmall

Stenger, M. (2014, December 17). Why curiosity enhances learning. *Edutopia.* https://www.edutopia.org/blog/why-curiosity-enhances-learning-marianne-stenger

Tiret, H. (2025, February 19). *Effects of excessive screen time on adults.* Michigan State University Extension: Healthy Relationships. https://www.canr.msu.edu/news/digital_technology_and_mental_health

World Health Organization. (2024, September 25). *Teens, screens, and mental health.* https://www.who.int/europe/news/item/25-09-2024-teens--screens-and-mental-health

Index

CORWIN

To help every educator help every student

We believe that every single student deserves a great education

We believe that knowing our impact is both a privilege and a responsibility

We believe that a fair, stable, and thriving society is built on education

Zeitfracht Medien GmbH
Ferdinand-Jühlke-Straße 7
99095 Erfurt, Deutschland
produktsicherheit@kolibri360.de